Style Therapy

30 DAYS TO YOUR SIGNATURE STYLE

— by —

LAUREN MESSIAH

ABRAMS IMAGE, NEW YORK

30-Day Style Therapy Checklist

Your Signature Style Awaits

Introduction

Do you love the way you look right now? Are you feeling like a ten on the confidence scale? If you ran into an ex-boyfriend, an old friend, or a client, would you be embarrassed because of your appearance?

Do you feel comfortable in your clothes or are you dying to get out of them by the end of the day? Or maybe you're a little too comfortable because they're baggy and oversized?

What's the state of your closet? Is that "clothes chair" in your bedroom stacked high with your failed outfit attempts? Have you recently experienced a "closet meltdown"? You know, a wild outburst that would shock a toddler, because you can't find anything to wear.

Do you love everything in your closet or just a measly 20 percent?

I hope you didn't answer yes to any of these questions, but something tells me you did. Now I want you to envision your new reality.

You spring out of bed, fling open your closet doors, and feel inspired. You love everything hanging in your closet. The outfit possibilities are endless. You feel sexy, cool, and confident because you have the exact clothes you need for all of the important areas of your life.

This could be you.

I know getting dressed can be hard work. Sometimes picking out a stylish outfit gets so frustrating that it's easier to say, "Style is dumb and superficial. People should like me for me." They <u>should</u> like you for you, but real life is more complicated than that.

In order for people to like you, trust you, spend money with you, or date you, they need to get to know you first. How you look and what you wear is like the trailer to a great movie: The world needs to be enticed by your trailer before they watch the movie.

Plus, word on the street is it takes less than seven seconds for a person to form an opinion about you. Seven seconds isn't enough time to win people over with your personality. Let's get real. People are judging you by your looks, and this may sound crazy, but this is good news.

The way you dress is 100 percent in your control, which means you get to change the narrative. You get to fully express your best and most powerful self through your personal style.

You get to start dressing like the woman you were meant to be right now. You can look (and feel) polished and put together, without looking like you tried too hard. But, more important, you can dress for the life you want. I've dressed my way into career success, body confidence, and even into romantic relationships.

Style is a powerful tool that can change your life, and that's exactly what you're going to do over the next thirty days.

Confession Time

Believe it or not, I'm a hard-core introvert. For as long as I can remember I've struggled to express myself, speak up, and take up space in a room. People scared the crap out of me, and given the choice, I'd hang out with a pet over a person.

At five years old I learned how to sew, and the world of style opened up to me. I found that when I dressed up, I felt confident, people would talk to me, and I could finally express myself.

Style gave me life.

I went to college and earned my degree in fashion design. I had visions of running off to New York to become a designer, but the universe had other plans. As it turns out, designers don't make very much money and I very much wanted to move out of my parents' house. So I did what any fashion-obsessed, college-educated girl with no job prospects in sight does. I started working retail.

My retail job was one of the best things to happen to me because I realized design wasn't my calling; it was dressing people that brought me joy.

Cut to me at twenty-eight, working as a celebrity stylist in Hollywood. The glitz, the glamour, the fabulous people . . . didn't actually exist. To my surprise, working as a celebrity stylist was awful. The egos, the long hours, and the vanity of it all just wasn't for me.

Obviously, this realization bummed me out because I thought I'd finally found my calling, so I did some soul-searching. This is where my love for personal development was born. I read every book, went to every seminar (hey, Tony Robbins), and hired coaches to help make sense of my life.

Then my aha moment arrived.

I loved dressing people (just not celebrity people). I loved the internal and external results I experienced when I dug deeper into my psyche. What if I took what I learned as a Hollywood stylist, combined it with what I found on my personal development journey, and then applied it to everyday people?

Boom! A calling was born.

Do the Work

Style Therapy _is a_ _workbook_ _designed to help you dis-_ _cover yourself and your authentic sense of style. In_ _other words, your signature style._

Notice how the word "workbook" is underlined? I did that on purpose. I wanted to emphasize the work aspect of this book.

I'm not your average stylist, you see. I'm not here to tell you exactly what to wear and dress you up like a little paper doll. My job is to serve as your guide through the most epic style journey you'll ever go on.

Over the next thirty days you are going to tap into the depth of your freaking soul and develop a sense of style that is unique to you.

When we go shopping and get dressed, an internal dialogue kicks in. What comes to the surface are old stories centered around money issues, body issues, low self-esteem, and relationship issues. That nonsense, coupled with a lack of basic styling principles, is the thing preventing you from looking your best and pursuing your true potential.

Enough is enough. It's time to look like you, only better. That means choosing the right clothes, sure. But it also means choosing new words to describe yourself, what you want to accomplish, and how you want to be perceived.

This is going to involve some work on your part. When I challenge you to do something, do it. When you are prompted to write, write.

Do the work. Get the results. Period.

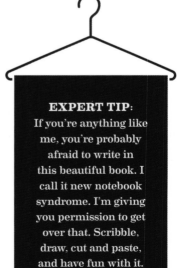

EXPERT TIP:
If you're anything like me, you're probably afraid to write in this beautiful book. I call it new notebook syndrome. I'm giving you permission to get over that. Scribble, draw, cut and paste, and have fun with it.

Building Your Signature Style

I have a fun little formula that I'd like you to keep in mind as we go through this process. It summarizes how all the daily exercises come together:

Character + Body Confidence + Goals
=
Your Signature Style

Character

I'm talking about looking at who you are on the inside. Your interests, priorities, tastes, and day-to-day life are the foundational building blocks of your personal style. Yes, we're going for a style transformation, but the underlying result is to have you looking and feeling even more like yourself.

Goals

You'll start to visualize how you want to grow and translate that vision into clothes that help you step into that role. Maybe you've already accomplished so much, but sense that you aren't living up to your full potential or aren't being perceived for your full worth. Style is an incredibly powerful tool in shaping the narrative.

Body Confidence

You'll make a commitment to work with your body exactly as it is right now! We all have to put on clothes, we all have to live in our bodies, and we all deserve to be seen. I know from experience that changing our relationship with clothing can truly shift the way we feel about ourselves—and that includes our bodies!

Signature Style

A signature style is the ultimate expression of self-awareness. It's the outer manifestation of your inner work. By the end of this process, you'll be putting together outfits that serve your day-to-day life, boost your self-confidence, and support your aspirations—woo hoo!

WEEK

01

Start
Where
You Are

Started from the bottom now we're here.

A wise man once said, "Started from the bottom now we're here."

That wise man was Drake.

You've got to admit: He makes an excellent point. Where you start doesn't necessarily dictate where you're going. I mean, he started at the bottom, and now he's Drake. Not a Drake fan? Fine. Look at Oprah. She started with less than nothing, and now she's freaking Oprah!

Now let's get stylish with it.

Take any modern-day style icon, and then take a gander at photos of them before they were stars. They started from the bottom too.

Week 1 is about creating your own "before" picture. You'll also uncork the underlying motivation that is going to drive your style transformation. So, whether you're a style train wreck, in need of a little tune-up, or taking your style to the next level, your style icon status awaits you.

Style Your Mind

Is there anything more satisfying than looking back at how far you've come?

My mind goes straight to the disgusting shared college dorm bathroom with cockroaches that were ready and willing to take a life if push came to shove. Then I think about my current bathroom situation. Sure, it's in desperate need of a remodel, but it's mine, and I bought it with my hard-earned money. Without that quick glance into the past, it's easy to hate on my current bathroom with its super-scary 1990s Jacuzzi tub, and hard for me to appreciate how far I've come.

The same goes for your style. Sometimes you can't appreciate how awesome you look without seeing how rough you were looking before. Which is why this week is devoted to documenting your "before." We'll do this through a series of selfies, and a healthy dose of self-reflection.

Now, I'm going to go out on a limb here and assume you're like 99 percent of my clients, who are terrified of selfies. Trust me; I get it. The word "selfie" often conjures up mental imagery of bikini-clad Instagram models serving duck face like it's their job! Well, technically, it is their job, but I digress.

I want you to erase that mental image. Clear it right away, because this week we are going to think about selfies in a fresh new way: as a means for self-reflection and empowerment.

EXPERT TIP:
Use your cell phone to take your selfies and print them out using an instant printer like the HP Sprocket.

Are you ready? OK, let's do this!

The 7-Day Selfie Challenge

For the next seven days, I want you to take full-on (and full-length) mirror selfies. Don't get all dressed up for this; it isn't a competition, and it certainly isn't a fashion show. The goal is to get an accurate representation of what you're wearing each day.

Next, you'll write a brief description of what you wore, how you felt, and how you were perceived. Before you get started, I want to clarify the word "perceived." This does not mean compliments, but certainly document them if you get some. Take notice of how people are reacting to you throughout the day. Were people opening doors for you and smiling? Or were they completely ignoring you? Did you get an extra muffin at the bakery? Be an observer, and then reflect on how your appearance may or may not have contributed to those reactions.

This process is crucial to your style transformation, so don't you dare try to skip it. Bust past the fear, all of your preconceived ideas, and just do it. My clients have walked away with some serious aha moments after completing this challenge. I do this challenge at least twice a year as a way to check in on myself and my style.

In addition to your daily selfies, each day you'll be tasked with a mind-set prompt to prepare you and motivate you mentally. Remember, you're embarking upon a total transformation by approaching style from the inside out, which means we've got to style the mind, too.

You've got this, girl! Now go on and snap some selfies.

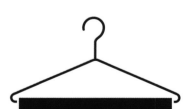

EXPERT TIP:
If you don't own a full-length mirror at this point, run—don't walk—out to get one immediately!

Lauren's Selfie Challenge

WHAT I WORE:

Vintage Metallica tee, Ganni sequin wrap dress worn as a duster, Frame jeans, Stuart Weitzman booties, Rag & Bone belt, pearl hair clip from Amazon

SELFIE:

HOW I FELT:

I felt cool, confident, and completely authentic. The sequin dress as a jacket was a risk, but I'm glad I took it because it ended up working out. Loved the white booties. I almost didn't buy them, but I'm so happy I did because they are so comfortable and versatile.

HOW I WAS PERCEIVED:

The man at the paint store was shockingly nice to me — he's usually pretty cranky (I've been spending a lot of time at the paint store due to my home remodel). I posted this outfit on Instagram, and I was applauded for my creativity with the dress-turned-duster trick.

Set Your Intention

What does success look like for you at the end of this process?

That's the first question I ask my clients during our initial styling consultation. Without a specific intention, your style success is like a moving target. But when my clients can imagine their style success and clearly articulate it to me, the end result is pure magic.

Now, I know I've thrown the term "style success" around a couple of times without bothering to define it, so let's do that right now.

STYLE SUCCESS SCENARIO #1:

Freak-Out-Free Mornings

If your current morning routine includes a blank stare into your closet, freaking out, and then reaching for that go-to pair of jeans (you know the pair), then freak-out-free mornings might be your idea of style success. I want you to visualize what a freak-out-free morning looks like for you. I imagine it could look a little something like this:

You wake up (without your alarm), excited to start your day. After a refreshing shower, you put on your cozy robe and assume the position in front of your closet. With a smile on your face, you open the closet doors. Every garment makes you happy and fits you well, and you know exactly how to wear each piece. You select a winning outfit in five minutes flat, do your hair/makeup, and then you're out the door with time to spare.

STYLE SUCCESS SCENARIO #2:

A "Love Your Body" Wardrobe

If the phrases "Nothing ever fits me!" and "Do I look fat in this?" regularly leave your lips, then your style success may hinge upon your ability to create a wardrobe that helps you love your body no matter what size it is. Let's paint the picture:

After a long day at the office, your husband surprises you with dinner reservations at a trendy new restaurant. You'd normally freak out on him because "Helloooo? Can I get some advance notice?" but not this time. You have the perfect date-night outfit hanging in your closet. No more pre-dinner "Do I look fat in this?" arguments, which are a real buzzkill. Instead, you have a lovely dinner and the rest of the evening goes quite well too (if you know what I'm saying).

EXPERT TIP: Not sure what exactly you want to accomplish on Day 1? Pay attention to how you feel throughout the 7-Day Selfie Challenge and come back to this question later.

STYLE SUCCESS SCENARIO #3:

Increased Confidence

If you dream of pulling off some seriously daring outfits but instead pull on some seriously sad leggings, then a lack of style confidence might be your issue. This can only mean one thing: A big ole shot of confidence will be your ticket to style success. So what does unstoppable confidence look like? It could look just like this:

You walk into a crowded room with your head held high and your heels higher. In a sea of boring LBDs, you're rocking a dress in a vibrant color with a bold print. You used to be the girl in the little black dress, but your printed dress matches your personality so much more. This is crazy: You were once a wallflower, and now you're the life of the party! If you had a dollar for each time someone complimented your outfit, you'd be swimming in money like Scrooge McDuck.

My imagination goes a bit wild sometimes. So if those style success scenarios didn't resonate with you, try one of these on for size:

- Ditching your "don't look at me" all-black wardrobe for something more colorful

- Adding some personality to your look with jewelry and accessories

- Getting your sexy back by showing some skin and attracting love into your life

- Being taken more seriously at work and scoring a big fat raise

- A self-love increase because when you look good, you feel good

- Becoming a better example for your kids, especially your daughters

Set Your Intention

SHORT-TERM GOAL: What does style success look like for you at the end of the thirty days?

_____

_____

_____

_____

_____

_____

LONG-TERM GOAL: What does style success look like for you in the long run?

_____

_____

_____

_____

_____

_____

VISUALIZE IT: Picture yourself in one of your "after" outfits. Describe how you look and feel.

_____

_____

_____

_____

_____

_____

Selfie Challenge

DATE: /   /

WHAT I WORE:

SELFIE:

HOW I FELT:

HOW I WAS PERCEIVED:

Let's Get Motivated

The fastest way to push a "should" into action is a darn good reason. For example, I "should" cook more instead of ordering Postmates fifty-five times a week. But without a good reason, like going into debt over a burrito bowl habit, I'm not going to stop.

The same goes for style. You can want to look polished and put together all day, but without a good reason to follow through, you will inevitably slip back into your boring jeans and T-shirt habit.

Some of you may already know your reason; in fact, it's probably why you picked up this workbook. As for the rest of you, we need to tap into what's motivating you to make a lasting change.

All of this "good reason" talk has me thinking about my client Shannon.

Shannon called me up because she needed a dress for a movie premiere. Truth be told, I can't stand these types of styling jobs. To me, styling one outfit is like putting a Band-Aid on a bullet hole. You see, Shannon's style was a mess and one nice dress wasn't going to fix her. But, just as any good drug dealer would do, I decided to give her a taste of the good stuff just to get her hooked.

She walked the red carpet in a gorgeous dress and felt the true power of unstoppable confidence. She looked good and no one could tell her any different. I was happy for her, even though I knew her style hangover was right around the corner. You can't go from looking like Cinderella at the ball one night to looking like a pumpkin the next and be OK with it!

Shannon lasted a few weeks in her pre-ball wardrobe before calling me again. "Lauren! Everyone at work thinks I'm a PA (production assistant) and I think it's because of my wardrobe."

The reason, which was there all along, suddenly presented itself in vibrant Technicolor. Just one night in the right clothes allowed people to see Shannon in a different light. Heck, she saw herself in a different light too. So when she stepped back into the darkness, the contrast was startling. Was her appearance the reason she being passed up for game-changing opportunities at work? Homegirl had herself a good reason, a real reason—her career and overall happiness were in jeopardy if she didn't make a change.

Making money and kicking butt in your career aren't the only reasons to change your style. Here are a few other reasons to think about as you prepare for today's assignment:

- Finding love or putting the passion back into your current relationship

- Getting out of a funk and improving your overall happiness

- Having clothes that actually feel like YOU so you can rock on with your authentic self

Before you dive into the work, let me quickly clarify the difference between intention and motivation. Intention is *what* you want to do/have. Motivation is *why* you must do it.

Find Your Real Reason

SPILL IT: What is the motivation behind your style transformation?

_____

_____

_____

_____

_____

_____

_____

GO DEEPER: Outside of looking better, what is the real reason you want to change your style?

_____

_____

_____

_____

_____

_____

_____

Selfie Challenge

DATE: /   /

WHAT I WORE:

_____

_____

_____

_____

_____

SELFIE:

HOW I FELT:

_____

_____

_____

_____

_____

HOW I WAS PERCEIVED:

_____

_____

_____

_____

_____

Go Deep. Go Dark.

If we were watching a movie, this would be the part where the dark clouds roll in and the narrator says, "What happens if you don't improve your style?" in a deep, creepy-sounding voice.

I've been asking my prospective clients this question for over a decade because it allows me to gauge how serious they are about improving their style. If their answer is, "I don't know? Nothing," I know the makeover won't stick. They don't have any skin in the game.

Now, if they take it to the dark place, I have something to work with.

I swore that I had invented this "take it to the dark place" line of questioning. As it turns out, Charles Dickens did. Remember A Christmas Carol? Ebenezer Scrooge is able to change only after seeing that his past and present actions have set him on a course toward a horrible future.

The NLP (neuro-linguistic programming) crowd has adapted this process in order to get people to visualize multiple paths. Tony Robbins is a big fan of the Dickens Process and he took me through it during his Unleash the Power Within seminar. I finally experienced firsthand how powerful the exercise can be.

I want you to take a trip down the rabbit hole. What happens if you never improve your style? Will you be stuck in your dead-end job forever because the woman with style and confidence keeps getting your promotion? Will you continue putting your dreams and desires on a shelf because you "have to" take care of everyone else first?

I know those scenarios are uncomfortable to hear—heck, they are uncomfortable to write—but we both know the stakes are higher than they might seem.

Confession Time

Let me take you on a vacation. A vacation to the arctic tundra called my love life. I was days away from earning my master's degree in being single. Seriously, I had been single for *years* without a prospect in sight. To me, this was a real head-scratcher because, *hello, I'm awesome.*

I did a little digging, I snapped some selfies, and I spent a considerable amount of time in a state of reflection. That's when it hit me! Holy cow, I was dressing pretty darn masculine. Plus, I'd cut off all of my hair and I rarely left the house. Real talk, I looked like a teenage boy with very expensive taste.

Couple that with unresolved feelings of unworthiness and a pile of past relationship trauma that I casually swept under the rug, and I had the perfect recipe for being single.

You'd think that realization would jolt me into a state of massive action, but it didn't. To the casual observer it seemed like the perfect opportunity to fire up the dating apps, pop on a dress, and get busy. But there I sat on my couch, dog on my lap, Netflix playing in the background, as I mindlessly scrolled through Instagram living the antithesis of the dream.

I had no choice but to take it to the dark place, because it was clear I'd become quite comfy in my boyfriend jeans and a perpetual state of singleness.

What would happen if I never changed? What if every single day for the rest of my life I wore my baggy jeans and Guns N' Roses T-shirt, ate takeout, and worked the night away on my laptop? Would two years of being single turn into three? Would three years turn into ten years? Would ten years turn into me dying alone, then having my dog eat my rotting brains for dinner? (C'mon, I warned you about my overactive imagination on day one.)

I decided to stop repelling the opposite sex with my style and focused on tapping into my suppressed feminine energy instead.

And guess what: It worked. My milkshake was actively bringing all the boys back to the yard (what, not a Kelis fan?), and now I embrace my feminine power in a way I hadn't before.

Go Deep. Go Dark.

VISUALIZE IT: What happens if you don't improve your style?

_____

_____

_____

_____

_____

_____

_____

EXPAND ON IT: What are the negative consequences outside of not looking the way you really want and staying stuck?

_____

_____

_____

_____

_____

_____

_____

_____

Selfie Challenge

DATE: ____ / ____ / ____

WHAT I WORE:

_____

_____

_____

_____

_____

SELFIE:

HOW I FELT:

_____

_____

_____

_____

_____

HOW I WAS PERCEIVED:

_____

_____

_____

_____

_____

Change Your Style Change Your Life

The Ripple Effect

Whew! We made it out of the dark place and are stepping back into the light. Instead of taking things to the dark place (been there, done that), we are exploring the positive impact this style transformation will have on your life. I like to call this the "ripple effect"—another concept I wish I made up but totally didn't. So instead of taking it to the dark place, we are taking it to the happy place.

If you haven't noticed by now, I'm dead serious when it comes to style. The clothes you put on your back have superpowers. The right outfit can make you feel unstoppable, sexy, smart, powerful, or all of the above. When you feel good, good things are bound to happen.

Take Heidi, one of my virtual clients, who was skeptical about stepping up her office attire. I challenged her to dress up her standard jeans and T-shirt by adding a classic black blazer. She listened (like a good client should) and the results blew her mind.

"I was in my boss's office and all of a sudden she said, 'Hey! I wanted to say I've noticed you've been dressing really nice lately. Love those blazers you're wearing—looks good!'"

This interaction started a dialogue around Heidi's future with the company and her career aspirations. Apparently, Heidi and her boss rarely see eye to eye, so this conversation about a blazer was huge. Who knows, six months from now Heidi may have her boss's job!

That is one example of the power of the "ripple effect." I live for these stories. The right outfit can lead you to your dream job, your soul mate, or your new best friend.

Preview the "After"

PREDICT IT: What is one possible outcome of your style transformation?

EXPAND IT: Imagine the "ripple effect" of the positive outcome above; spare no details.

Selfie Challenge

DATE: /   /

WHAT I WORE:

_____

_____

_____

_____

_____

SELFIE:

HOW I FELT:

_____

_____

_____

_____

_____

HOW I WAS PERCEIVED:

_____

_____

_____

_____

_____

Charging Through Challenges

Don't you hate it when you're moving right along and then out of the blue something stands in your way? It's kind of like driving. One second you're cruising down the street, singing along to your favorite tunes, and then BAM! Standstill traffic. It's annoying, but you don't turn around and go back home every time you hit traffic, do you? No. You sit there, get through it, and eventually arrive at your destination. It was a minor inconvenience that you had to overcome to get to where you wanted to go.

I'm telling you this now so you don't freak out later. You *will* hit some traffic on this style journey, but guess what: You'll get through it. I promise.

I was chatting with my hypnotherapist the other day (shut up, I'm an LA person; I have a hypnotherapist), and I was going on and on about how life was so darn stressful. Without going into too much detail, our interaction went kind of like this:

"I got this (enter awesome thing here), but I have to (enter moderately hard thing here) or else (enter horrible doomsday scenario here) will happen."

Then she said, "It sounds like everything in your life is great, but you're just choosing to see the potential for negative instead of the positive reality."

Oh snap! This is why I pay her the big bucks. My hypnotherapist was right. All of these good things are on the horizon, but I was choosing to magnify potential challenges in an effort to self-sabotage.

I see my clients do this ALL the time with their style. They are a beautiful blank canvas just waiting to be painted. Then here it comes: ***But, Lauren . . .*** These are all of the challenges that, in the past, stopped them dead in their tracks from improving their style.

But, Lauren, my thighs are too big.

But, Lauren, you don't understand: Nothing ever fits me.

But, Lauren, it's too hot and humid where I live to dress cute.

But, Lauren, I'm broke and can't afford nice clothes.

But, Lauren, I wear a uniform at work so what's the point?

But, Lauren, I have really skinny ankles.

But, Lauren, I have kids and they need clothes more than I do.

But, Lauren, I work from home so what's the point of getting dressed?

But, Lauren, everyone else at the office wears jeans and T-shirts.

But, Lauren, I'm retired.

I could go on all freaking day repeating sentences that start with ***"But, Lauren."*** The point is, I've heard every excuse out there and they are just that . . . excuses.

Shall I remind you what an excuse is? Actually, I will, because the definition of an excuse legit cracks me up: "a reason or explanation put forward to defend or justify a fault or offense."

Stop trying to defend your existing style. You don't like it, so let's change it.

Oops, Tough Love Lauren just arrived without warning. I'm not at all trying to minimize your pain and struggles. They can feel very real and legitimate. My point is that change is possible. I've worked through every style challenge in the book. We'll dive deep into those challenges next week, but right now I want you to unload.

Turn the page and give me all of your excuses, because sometimes you just need to get the poison out of your head and onto paper.

Go Ahead and Vent

LET IT OUT: In the past, what has stood in your way when it comes to improving your style? Was it a body-related issue, your finances, or worrying about other people's opinions?

Whatever it is, write it out and don't hold back.

Selfie Challenge

WHAT I WORE:

_____

_____

_____

_____

SELFIE:

HOW I FELT:

_____

_____

_____

_____

HOW I WAS PERCEIVED:

_____

_____

_____

_____

Take Inventory

Early in my career, I had a closet full of statement pieces and none of the basics that would maximize all of the fun stuff I was buying. Instead of just wearing the crazy graphic tee with jeans, I realized that I could upgrade my outfit by adding a classic black blazer, or tucking that tee inside a black pencil skirt for a casual date night ensemble. This "duh" moment (and my love of lists) birthed the "Ultimate Wardrobe Checklist."

The Ultimate Wardrobe Checklist

BASICS

Jackets and Coats

[ ] Leather Biker Jacket
[ ] Denim Jacket
[ ] Blazer
[ ] Tuxedo Jacket
[ ] Camel Coat
[ ] Trench Coat
[ ] Double-Breasted Wool Coat

Knits

[ ] Chunky Sweater
[ ] Cashmere V-Neck
[ ] Sweatshirt
[ ] Hoodie
[ ] Crewneck Sweater
[ ] Long Cardigan
[ ] Black Turtleneck

Tops and Blouses

[ ] White Cotton Shirt
[ ] Black Camisole
[ ] White Tee
[ ] Silk Blouse
[ ] Evening Blouse
[ ] Chambray Top
[ ] Striped Tee

Pants and Bottoms

[ ] Wide-Leg Pants
[ ] Skinny Jeans
[ ] Boyfriend Jeans
[ ] Leather Pants
[ ] Cigarette Pants
[ ] Leggings
[ ] Flare Jeans
[ ] Denim Shorts
[ ] Cropped Pants
[ ] Suit Pants

Skirts

[ ] Pencil Skirt
[ ] A-line Skirt
[ ] Miniskirt
[ ] Midi Skirt
[ ] Maxi Skirt

Dresses

[ ] Little Black Dress
[ ] Power Dress
[ ] Summer Dress
[ ] Boho-Style Dress
[ ] Day Dress
[ ] Wrap Dress
[ ] Cocktail Dress
[ ] Evening Dress

Shoes

[ ] Block-Heel Shoe
[ ] Heeled Sandal
[ ] High-Heeled Pump (Black)

EXPERT TIP:
Check off all of the pieces
you own that fit and are in
good condition. Highlight
the items that you are
missing and feel you need
to add to your wardrobe.

[ ] High-Heeled Pump (Nude)
[ ] Knee-High Boots
[ ] Ankle Boots
[ ] Loafers
[ ] Fancy Flat
[ ] White Sneakers
[ ] Espadrille
[ ] Summer Sandals

Bags

[ ] Cross-Body Bag
[ ] Chain-Strap Bag
[ ] Clutch
[ ] Tote Bag
[ ] Bucket Bag
[ ] Structured Bag
[ ] Quilted Bag

Jewelry

[ ] Architectural Earrings
[ ] Statement Earrings
[ ] Gold Hoop Earrings

[ ] Diamond Studs
[ ] Cocktail Ring
[ ] Delicate Rings
[ ] Classic Wristwatch
[ ] Cuff
[ ] Gold Bangle
[ ] Statement Necklace
[ ] Pearl Necklace
[ ] Delicate Necklace

Accessories

[ ] Leather Belt
[ ] Waist-Cinching Belt
[ ] Cashmere Scarf
[ ] Silk Scarf
[ ] Wayfarer Shades
[ ] Baseball Hat
[ ] Fedora
[ ] Straw Hat
[ ] Wrap
[ ] Aviator Sunglasses

STATEMENT PIECES

[ ] Evening Ankle Boots
[ ] Statement Pumps
[ ] Statement Skirt
[ ] Playful Clutch
[ ] Fur Coat
[ ] Tweed Jacket
[ ] Graphic Tee
[ ] Statement Jacket
[ ] Beaded Top
[ ] Culottes
[ ] Printed Pants
[ ] Evening Jumpsuit
[ ] Bodysuit
[ ] Bomber Jacket
[ ] Kimono Jacket
[ ] Animal-Print Blouse

Confession Time

There is nothing more insulting than being asked to grab coffee for everyone at a business meeting when you're the freaking business owner! Oh wait, yes, there is: tacking the word "sweetie" onto the request *and* asking if I had my pen and notebook handy for note taking.

This was my life at thirty. I was running a multiple six-figure business with a male business partner. We had a big meeting with a Hollywood agent that I was very excited about, and I was being treated like an entry-level chump.

My default was to blame the system. This big-time Hollywood agent *would* treat a woman this way, especially a woman of color. While that certainly could've been at play, I decided to do some style self-reflection. All of my outfits in their casual yet over-the-top glory flashed before my eyes. Duh! Of course, everyone thought I was an assistant. I wasn't even close to dressing the part of a business boss.

Once I saw the light, it was impossible to unsee it. I asked myself, what would a successful business owner (one who doesn't get asked to fetch coffee) wear? I changed my style and changed the way I showed up for my business. Within a year's time I had accelerated my business from six figures to seven figures, and I felt more confident and powerful. I hopped off the struggle bus and hitched a ride on the success train.

Lauren at work before her makeover.

Lauren at work after her makeover (no longer fetching coffee).

Selfie Challenge

DATE: /   /

WHAT I WORE:

_____

_____

_____

_____

_____

SELFIE:

HOW I FELT:

_____

_____

_____

_____

_____

HOW I WAS PERCEIVED:

_____

_____

_____

_____

_____

Reflections and Aha Moments

Look at you, surviving a week of taking selfies! Hopefully the process got easier as you went along. The 7-Day Selfie Challenge happens to be my favorite part of the styling process because it's so darn revealing. It's funny what you see once you start paying attention.

I remember chatting with my client Rachel about her 7-Day Selfie Challenge experience. I expected her to say something about the fact that she was drowning in her clothes, or that the colors she was rocking washed her out. She saw those things, but she also saw something much deeper.

Rachel's family has a long history of health issues, from heart disease to other unsavory ailments. This was something Rachel never really thought about in regard to her own health—those were her family's problems. However, after looking in the mirror for seven straight days, she noticed she looked a bit tired.

Rachel visited the doctor and learned that the health issues that plagued her family were now her problem too. This lit a fire under her booty. Rachel started taking better care of her health by getting more rest and more exercise and making better food choices. Today Rachel has a clean bill of health and it all started with the selfie challenge.

If that isn't an aha moment, then I clearly don't know the definition of "aha."

What did you see when you looked in the mirror? Your realization doesn't have to be as extreme as my client's; it could be a simple as:

- My client Christy, who noticed the better she dressed the friendlier people acted toward her

- Or Victoria, who noticed she was speeding through life and needed to give herself more time to not only get dressed in the morning but to "stop and smell the roses"

- How about Laurie, who noticed her boxy clothing wasn't doing her any favors and she was actually hiding to avoid unwanted male attention

Selfie Challenge

DATE: /   /

WHAT I WORE:

_____

_____

_____

_____

_____

SELFIE:

HOW I FELT:

_____

_____

_____

_____

_____

HOW I WAS PERCEIVED:

_____

_____

_____

_____

_____

A Time for Reflection

On a scale from 1–10, how happy were you with your outfits?

1   2   3   4   5   6   7   8   9   10

Describe your current style in three words:

1. _____

2. _____

3. _____

Do those three words represent who you are?

_____

_____

_____

_____

_____

_____

_____

What was your favorite outfit of the week? Why?

What was your least favorite of the week? Why?

Did you feel overdressed or underdressed at any point during the week?

DAY 7: DO THE WORK

Look back at your selfies—how well did your clothes fit?

_____

_____

_____

_____

_____

_____

_____

_____

Overall, how comfortable were you in your outfits?

_____

_____

_____

_____

_____

_____

_____

_____

What message do you think your overall appearance was sending?

_____

_____

_____

_____

_____

_____

How easy was it to get dressed each morning?

_____

_____

_____

_____

_____

_____

Did you experience any aha moments during the challenge? If so, let's hear all about them.

_____

_____

_____

_____

_____

WEEK

02

**Clear
Your
Path**

Free your mind and the rest will follow.

*In the immortal words of En Vogue: "Free your mind
and the rest will follow."*

If you'd told sixth-grade Lauren, who was happily
jamming in her room to En Vogue, that she would later
create a style philosophy around that lyric, I wouldn't
have believed you. But dang it, the R & B ladies were
onto something, because your mind is the biggest ob-
stacle standing between you and your signature style.

Yep, that big, beautiful brain of yours is messing with
your style mojo.

Week 2 is all about clearing the roadblocks that are
keeping you away from your fabulous. You'll toss away
the bad programming that has been limiting your
greatness.

It's time to get out of your own way and tidy up that
internal clutter so we can clear your path.

Now grab a flashlight because we're going in.

Style Roadblocks

I need you to stand tall and go deep during this next stretch of your style journey. Why? Because it's impossible to fill your closet with clothing you love if your mind is cluttered with self-limiting beliefs.

It's time to get out of your own way and clear the cobwebs of your past. Because as fun as it is to blame other people for your less than stylish situation, at the end of the day you get to decide if you're going to let those rotten memories from your past fester a little longer.

This means revisiting moments like the time in the dressing room when you needed the next size up and the snooty salesgirl said, "Sorry, we don't carry that size." From then on you swore you had to be a certain size to be chic. Since you aren't that size yet (whatever that size is), you're still schlumping around town in "comfy" clothes.

Or that time when your mom commented on the fact that you seem to wear the same outfit over and over again. Ever since, you've never repeated an outfit even though it meant going into debt to stay stylish.

For the next seven days we're going to tackle the roadblocks standing in your way from fully expressing yourself through style.

This week isn't an easy one, but trust me: The hard work is worth it.

Confession Time

The year was 1995. I was in high school and grunge was the look, but I didn't have any trendy grunge clothing. While my classmates were swiping their parents' credit cards at Contempo Casuals, I was shopping at TJ Maxx, where the grunge look hadn't trickled down.

Desperate to fit in, I was willing to do whatever it took to get my hands on some grunge. I saved my babysitting money and headed straight to Kmart to buy some fresh threads. I know, I've come a long way.

I'll never forget the outfit I chose; it was so bad! I picked up this horrible oversized T-shirt that said, and I kid you not, *I was grunge before grunge was cool.* Did I mention the T-shirt had a cartoon bear on it? And the bear was wearing a flannel shirt? The target audience for this shirt was clearly *my dad,* but there I was at fifteen buying the bear shirt.

I wore that stupid shirt every single week for months! It was my Tuesday shirt (I was outfit planning before outfit planning was cool). And just as the bear did, I paired that T-shirt with an open flannel and jeans. Honestly, you couldn't tell me nothing, because I swore up and down that I was the coolest person in town. I genuinely looked forward to Tuesdays because I got to wear my "cool outfit" to school.

Then one day my mom said something about my outfit. In my memory she was screaming at me, but in reality, she was probably just like, "Hey, cool it with the old bear T-shirt."

Whatever way it went down, it hurt, and it also birthed a full-fledged shopaholic who was determined to never repeat an outfit ever again. I didn't know it then and I still didn't know it when I maxed out my AMEX at the tender age of twenty-six, but I was desperate for my mom's approval. I'd been trying to shop my way to unconditional love since the age of fifteen. Once I unearthed that traumatic little gem, I was able to throw it away and move on.

Other People's Opinions

Worrying about other people's opinions has been stopping greatness since the beginning of time. We want to be stylish, but the fear of "doing it wrong" and being judged by our peers stops us dead in our tracks. What do we do? We play it safe. How do we feel? Inauthentic and weird.

How does that saying go? Dance like no one's watching. What would happen if you dressed like no one's watching? The only way to do that is to destroy your style-killing fears.

STYLE-KILLING FEAR #1
Trying Too Hard

Change is tough because it requires entering the unknown. When I enter uncharted territory, my first instinct is to imagine the worst-case scenario. Changing your style is no different. Even if you're going from ho-hum to freaking fabulous, it's completely natural to assume the outside world will react negatively.

Take my client Tara, for example. Her college-student style was scoring her snide remarks at the watercooler. Oh, did I mention Tara is a top entertainment executive who graduated from college more than thirty years ago? She needed to change, but her fear told her if she started dressing like an adult, her coworkers would think she was "trying too hard."

Her real fear was looking inauthentic. Looking different, in her mind, meant becoming a totally different person.

STYLE-KILLING FEAR #2
Looking Too Old (or Too Young)

Aging is funny: We want to live forever, but we freak out every time we celebrate a birthday. This toxic relationship with aging messes with our style.

I'll never forget my client Callie. A beautiful woman in her forties who had it all: a hot young husband, a big house, and an even bigger career. She also had some self-esteem issues. Within ten seconds of meeting her, I knew she'd trip an old lady to be first in line at the fountain of youth.

When I presented her with wardrobe options (contemporary tweed jackets, silk blouses, shift dresses), her response was "Nope! Lauren, I'm not a grandma." Callie was only interested in body-con dresses, slinky camisoles, and tight jeans. All the things a forty-something executive should <u>not</u> wear to the office. Her fear of looking old had swung her into "desperate to look young" land.

STYLE-KILLING FEAR #3
Flaunting Too Much

"If you've got it, flaunt it!" Easier said than done. Whether it's a flaunt-worthy body or a bank account that would make Oprah jealous, celebrating your success can feel awkward because most of us have been conditioned to dim our light.

Over the course of my career I've come across my fair share of "modest millionaire" clients. Modesty is A-OK. Just because you have money doesn't mean you're required to show if off. But going full-on cheap? That has negative consequences too.

My client Nikki had plenty of money to invest in her wardrobe, but she thought spending money on expensive clothing wasn't right. The problem was Nikki loved designer fashion. Instead of being true to herself, she purchased a <u>ton</u> of fast fashion. She was spending the same amount of money on clothing she didn't love to protect herself from other people's opinions.

If those style-killing scenarios didn't resonate with you, give these fear-inducing assumptions a whirl:

- Dress better than everyone at work? People will think you're too ambitious.

- Stylish after a certain age? People will think you're desperate for attention.

- Rocking designer labels? People will think you're drowning in debt.

- Showing off your figure? People will think you aren't intelligent.

Can some of these opinions be true for some people? Yes, but that doesn't mean they are true for you. I want you to explore an outside opinion that's been holding you back from fully owning your style. Dig deep, because a lot of these thoughts were planted in your head years ago.

Write It Out

DESCRIBE IT: What opinions of others are holding you back?

FEEL IT: What about those opinions rings true for you?

EVALUATE IT: Is it possible that those opinions and your reaction to those opinions aren't based on truth?

_____

_____

_____

_____

_____

RATE IT: On a scale from 1–10, how ready are you to let those opinions go?

1   2   3   4   5   6   7   8   9   10

REJECT IT: What is one action you can take today to completely disregard that opinion?

_____

_____

_____

_____

_____

_____

_____

Body Confidence

One hundred percent of the clients I've worked with have some sort of body confidence issue. Did you hear me? I said 100 percent. That includes the super-svelte, the skinny, and the women with the perfectly placed curves.

I was talking to one of my stylist friends about celebrity body confidence and she said, "Hello, they're actresses! They're faking it." Meaning even celebrities—with their trainers, fancy organic food, and expensive beauty regimens—don't always love what they see in the mirror.

You're not unique. We've all got issues. Join the "I don't love my body" club. Actually, don't—because I've got good news: You can love and accept your body once you start to push past those boulder-sized roadblocks standing in your way.

When I was young, maybe twelve years old, my grandmother made a comment about how I looked in shorts. I believe her exact words were, "Oh my god, your legs are so fat in shorts!" I was shattered. It took me until I was thirty-six years old to wear shorts in public, all because my grandmother had made one comment.

To celebrate, I posted a photo on Instagram of me wearing shorts with my shorts-trauma tale in the caption. The number of positive comments from other women was mind-blowing. And to think

I roasted in the hot-hot heat for decades because one person didn't like how I looked in shorts.

Sharing my story helped take its power away. It wasn't about fishing for compliments; it was about healing. If I didn't put my body-shaming story out there, it would remain on a loop in my head. I imagined my story as a criminal doing push-ups in the prison yard, preparing to shank me in the shower. I didn't want to get shanked, so I picked up my weapons—pen, paper, a healthy dose of self-reflection—and I got to work.

Writing about it, talking about it, and looking at my legs with gratitude instead of judgment helped put things into perspective. Did my grandmother's words hurt? Yeah, of course. It took some serious work on my part to "get over" a passing comment, but the freedom and growth I experienced from it was well worth it. I was also able to forgive my grandmother. You know old people don't come with a filter.

I recently encouraged more than five thousand other women to take these steps during my annual Love Your Body Style Challenge. The pain these brave women worked through made my grandmother's shorts comment look like child's play. They talked about verbally abusive husbands, decades of negative commentary from their mothers, and years of being aggressively bullied in school.

These types of experiences morph into debilitating body issues that can take years of ongoing work to address. In the meantime, you need to wear clothes. Deciding that you deserve to dress your best right now, *regardless* of where you are in this process, is a profound step toward actually loving your body. I've seen it happen over and over again with my own two eyes.

EXPERT TIP:
When a negative thought pops in your head, I want you to say, "Nope! Try again." I do this *all the time*. Sounds insultingly simple, but it works. You'll run out of negative thoughts, and those buried empowering thoughts will be able to shine.

Love Your Body

REFLECT ON IT: Describe the moment when your relationship with your body turned from positive to negative.

_____

_____

_____

_____

_____

_____

_____

FOCUS ON IT: Find the positive, and describe a part of your body that you love and why you love it.

_____

_____

_____

_____

_____

_____

_____

_____

REDEFINE IT: Strip down and look in the mirror. Talk back to each piece of negative commentary that you've picked up from friends, family, and society. What is <u>your</u> definition of beauty?

DO IT: What are three things you can do to improve your relationship with your body?

1.

2.

3.

Money, Money, Money

Money and style are funny. If you don't have enough of the green stuff, then your lack of funds becomes the number one suspect in the "case of the missing style" mystery. On the flip side, when you have plenty of money, you end up trying to buy your way to great style. I think we both know that this is not how it works. Look at the Real Housewives: Money can't buy them sense or style.

As I started working with more and more clients, I noticed a pattern. The majority of my clients had a difficult time spending money on themselves. They wanted to get dressed in the cheapest way possible by accepting hand-me-downs that didn't complement their style, being a discount devotee, and wearing clothing down to the last thread.

I wanted to push them out of their comfort zone, so I made them check out places they couldn't afford. No one was buying anything; it was all for the luxury experience. My goal was for them to touch, feel, and experience beautifully designed and well-made clothing.

If you struggle with spending money on yourself, the following abundance exercise is for you.

Not everyone struggles with abundance; in fact, I've worked with quite a few clients who were straight-up fashion hoarders. Money wasn't a scarce resource, so their closet runneth over. If you are a self-professed shopaholic, skip the abundance exercise. I've got another activity for you.

We're all on a level playing field. Money or no money, you can look amazing. But you need to get clear on what put your funky money mentality in place. Then you can look like a million bucks in Target just as easily as you can in Gucci.

Confession Time

On the scale between big spending and frugality, I grew up somewhere in between. My parents complained about money nonstop. It always seemed like we were on the brink of financial ruin, but at the same time we lived in a big house that was constantly being remodeled or redecorated.

We were forever shopping for new clothes, but coupons were clipped and discount stores were frequented. Looking good and having new things was paramount. You just couldn't ever pay full price, or else you'd go broke and have to live under a bridge.

This ingrained a discount shopper chip into my brain. As an adult, no matter how much money I made, I'd beeline it straight to the clearance rack. I'd buy, buy, buy. Just not the stuff I truly loved. This resulted in an overstuffed closet with garments that didn't go together.

My money roadblock had to be cleared. I had created a box around my style, and inside this box I was selecting my visual identity from "whatever's left."

What kind of sad identity is that?

Visually, I was a collection of what didn't sell. Was I repeating this behavior in other areas of my life? Uh-huh. Sure was.

It only took about twenty seconds of reflection to realize that my love life was plucked straight out of a clearance bin. If a guy showed any amount of romantic interest, I was like, "Fine. I'll take it." Even if I didn't like him. The red flags were waving, but since I'd conditioned myself to choose from "whatever's left," these habits went completely unnoticed.

I was dating men I didn't like, and I was wearing clothes I didn't love. I was thinking small, and in my universe that won't do.

I had to reevaluate my approach to money, shopping, and obviously men, but let's stay focused on the task at hand—money.

If my intention behind shopping clearance was to save money, why didn't I exercise the other money-saving options I had available to me? Like, how about buying one full-priced garment that I really loved instead of purchasing ten mediocre clearance items? The truth is, I had never even considered it. But once I banished these roadblocks, everything changed for the better.

Abundance Exercise

If you are a devoted discount shopper, it's time to step outside of your bargain-imposed style box. Create a list of high-end stores you can visit in your city. Visit at least one of those stores. Drink the complimentary champagne, touch the clothes, try them on, and act like you belong there (because you do!).

DESCRIBE IT: What was your shopping experience like? Did you find anything that you loved?

_____

_____

_____

_____

_____

_____

REFLECT ON IT: Did you experience any aha moments or breakthroughs?

_____

_____

_____

_____

_____

_____

_____

RELATE IT: What was your relationship to "money and things" like growing up? Are there any old ideas you need to clear away?

RESOLVE IT: What are the new ideas you'd like to adopt instead?

Restraint Exercise

Are your closet space and your credit card completely maxed out? Instead of going shopping, I want you to shop your closet! Try on what you already have and create at least three new outfits. Then take some time to answer these questions.

FEEL IT: Do you feel like you have something to prove to someone else (i.e., your friends, your sister-in-law, the sales associates) while you're out shopping?

_____

_____

_____

_____

_____

_____

DESCRIBE IT: What is your emotional state before you go shopping? How do you feel after?

_____

_____

_____

_____

_____

_____

_____

RELATE IT: What was your relationship to "money and things" like growing up? Are there any old ideas you need to clear away?

RESOLVE IT: What are the new ideas you'd like to adopt instead?

Confronting the Ghosts of Your Past

I'm going to let you in on a little secret. I've had a long battle with the beast called perfectionism. Maybe I watched too much TV growing up, but in my mind things had to be perfect in order for me to be considered successful and worthy of love. If I did something wrong, that meant an invisible tick mark went into the undeserving column. The more "wrong" I did the more uneven the scales became, and when those scales were completely out of whack, the self-sabotage began.

I see this same self-destructive pattern happening with my clients. My client Sue knew exactly how she wanted to look and she even had some really nice pieces in her closet, but she still found herself reaching for her trusty purple T-shirt.

Why was she doing this? She knew what she wanted, she had what she wanted, but she couldn't pull herself away from this tee. I had to get to the bottom of this.

Sue told me that growing up people would constantly tell her she'd "be so pretty if she lost weight." She never lost the weight. She felt like she didn't deserve to look pretty, so she self-sabotaged herself by dressing down to meet other people's expectations.

I suggested she get rid of the shirt. Not just because it was ugly (it was) but because it clearly represented something deeper. The shirt was a style roadblock in physical form that was keeping her exactly where society thought a plus-size black woman should be. She knew better, and her accomplishments showed that. She's in her twenties, a homeowner, engaged to be married, and she has a successful career. And yet she's dressing like Sloppy Sue because she doesn't "deserve" to look cute? Nonsense.

When a garment carries that much emotional baggage, it deserves a proper send-off, and that's exactly what you're going to do.

What kind of baggage?
Here are a few examples:

- Holding on to a garment in hopes it will fit, but each time you try it on, you feel bad about yourself

- Keeping an item that doesn't suit you because you spent a ton of money on it and removing it from your closet is like admitting defeat

- Feeling guilty about parting with a garment because a loved one gave it to you.

How do you know if an item carries baggage? Well, it's kind of like the opposite of Marie Kondo's philosophy; instead "sparking joy," these garments spark despair, sadness, embarrassment, or regret.

I had this pair of black Stella McCartney pants in my closet. They were designer, fit perfectly, but for some reason I never wore them. I kept them because they were a classic, weren't taking up a lot of space, and surely someday I'd wear them.

EXPERT TIP:
You will be tempted to clean out your whole entire closet during this step. Don't do it! Trust the process. Your closet cleanse is coming on Day 14.

Years passed and still no love for the pants. Why couldn't I part with them?

I didn't want to admit defeat. In my perfectionist, big-time stylist mind, it made good sense to own classic black pants. I'd even used them as an example in a video. Getting rid of them meant I was wrong. Not just regular wrong, but career wrong. My entire identity was tied to be right in my professional life.

Today I'm happy to share that the pants are gone and being wrong didn't kill me.

Unpack Your Your Style Baggage

Write Your Style Eulogy

LET IT GO: Identify one item in your closet that carries emotional baggage. Write a style eulogy, because it's finally time to say goodbye.

Your Style Roadblock Action Plan

Today is all about building new patterns, because your style roadblocks *will* try to mess with you from time to time. They've been part of your programming for years—perhaps even decades. You have to create new habits, thoughts, and behaviors to meet your roadblocks head-on.

ROADBLOCK #1:
Other People's Opinions
Your personal roadblock related to Other People's Opinions is:

_____

_____

_____

_____

When this roadblock comes up, you will take the following actions:

_____

_____

_____

_____

_____

Example: I will spend five minutes each morning reciting positive affirmations.

ROADBLOCK #2:
Body Confidence
Your personal roadblock related to Body Confidence is:

_____

_____

_____

_____

When this roadblock comes up, you will take the following actions:

_____

_____

_____

_____

Example: I will start a body gratitude journal so I can stay aware of all of the great things my body has done for me and allows me to do.

ROADBLOCK #3:

Money

Your personal roadblock related to Money is:

_____

_____

_____

_____

_____

When this roadblock comes up, you will take the following actions:

_____

_____

_____

_____

_____

Example: I will focus on what I have instead of what I lack for one minute when scarcity thinking comes up.

Commit to Yourself

How committed are you to banishing these roadblocks?

_____

_____

How can you keep yourself accountable?

_____

_____

_____

How will you reward yourself for banishing these blocks?

_____

_____

Establishing Your 3 Words

When it comes to winning the game of life, you've got all sorts of handy tools at your disposal. Tools like your intellect, charisma, those pearly whites, and your network or connections.

There is another tool that's often neglected and ridiculed by many. I'm talking about style. Style can be used to influence people. Whether you're striving for a promotion, a partner, or some new friends, the way you dress can help you get there faster.

Style isn't about impressing other people; it's about influencing others so *you* can succeed. It's time to control the narrative and start using style to your advantage!

It all starts with three little words. It's a simple two-step process. Here is how it works:

Step 1: Choose three words that describe what you want people to know just by looking at you.

Step 2: Each time you get dressed and every time you shop, ask yourself if the clothes you're selecting embody those three words.

You can even have multiple sets of words for different areas of your life: for the office, for dating, or for momming around town. You get the point.

Let's take my client Rose. She was struggling with her style, her look was all over the place, and she didn't feel like she was seen properly at the office. She works as an executive assistant for a nonprofit and is considered the mother of the organization. I asked her what she thought her three words would be, and this is what she said:

1. Professional
2. Nurturing
3. Responsible

Those words are perfect guidance for her professional look. Just saying the words "professional," "nurturing," and "responsible" made it easier for her to put down the sparkly rhinestone belt when getting dressed for work. She can save that crazy belt for single-and-ready-to-mingle Rose.

Style is a Tool for Winning the Game of Life

Choosing Your 3 Words

LET IT OUT: If you need an on-ramp to expressing your style in three words, start by writing down how you want to feel and be perceived at work, at home, and when you're out socializing. Circle the keywords that emerge in this exercise.

_____

_____

_____

_____

_____

_____

_____

_____

_____

_____

_____

_____

_____

_____

_____

_____

WORKING. What are your three words for your professional wardrobe?

1. _____

2. _____

3. _____

HANGING OUT. What are your three words for your weekend wardrobe?

1. _____

2. _____

3. _____

SOCIALIZING. What are your three words for your social or going-out wardrobe?

1. _____

2. _____

3. _____

Clean Out Your Closet

This is one of the most exciting aspects of the styling process—it's time to make room for the new, more fabulous you! Everything you've done up to this point (Days 1–13) has been preparing you for this moment. When you walk into your closet with trash bags in hand, you have something you didn't have before: clarity.

STEP 1:

Phone a friend.

You now know how you want to be perceived and you're thinking about what needs to go in your closet (thanks to the Ultimate Wardrobe Checklist). You've identified the motivation that will move you forward and the roadblocks that could hold you back. You didn't have that last time you cleaned out your closet, and I'm guessing you accidentally got rid of everything you owned only to replace it with a bunch of stuff you don't love.

Before you get started, I want you to find your most honest friend. Can you clean out your closet alone? Sure. Should you do it alone? Absolutely not. Even with a head full of wisdom, all good sense flies out the window when it comes time to face the music. Review your style goals with your best bud and make sure they hold you accountable.

STEP 2:

Questions to ask

When debating whether or not you should get rid of a garment, ask yourself a few key questions:

ALIGNMENT QUESTIONS

- Does it support the overall vision for the woman I am becoming?

- Does it align with my three words?

QUALITY QUESTIONS

- Does it fit?

- Is it ripped, stained, or beyond repair?

- Does this piece have minor flaws that can easily be repaired?

- Does this item have sentimental value? Am I sure? If so, how important is it that I keep it?

STYLING QUESTIONS

- Can I wear this garment with at least three different outfits?

- When was the last time I wore this? Why has it been so long?

- Where can I wear this? The office, on a date, on the weekend?

STEP 3:

Divvy it up.

As you're wildly tossing items from your closet, make sure you're tossing them in the right place. Create the following piles, bags, or bins:

- **Keep.** These items stay in your closet and should be hung up on uniform hangers.

- **Tailor.** Items that need mending or can be altered into something you'd actually wear.

- **Consign/Sell.** If your closet is filled with designer and contemporary clothing in excellent condition, you may be sitting on a gold mine. Consign or sell those bad boys.

- **Donate.** These items aren't going to make you any money, but they could help someone in need. Find your favorite charity and make a donation.

- **Give to a friend.** If you have a friend who would benefit from your castoffs, hook her up!

- **Recycle.** Some items are beyond repair and are too gross to donate. Do some online research to find a textile recycling program—there are tons of options besides the landfill!

EXPERT TIP:
Fit is everything. If an item is too small, do yourself a favor and toss it. If an item you love is too big or the fit is a little off, take it to a trusted tailor before throwing in the towel. Check out my "Guide to Tailoring" on page 186.

WEEK
2

DAY
14

Merchandise Your Closet

Take what's left in your closet and make it look pretty, like a store. Do nice clothing boutiques have a pair of pajamas hanging next to a winter coat? No, they do not. All like items need to be hung or stacked together.

Long-Hanging Clothes

Designate one area of your closet for long garments. If possible, hang your outerwear in another closet to save space.

Short or Long Hanging Clothes

Depending on how your closet is configured, you can hang these items in the short area (if pants are folded over a hanger) or the long area (using hangers with clamps).

Closet Merchandising Guide

Coats
Long Coats
Trench Coats
Kimonos
Robes

Dresses/Jumpsuits
Gowns
Strapless Dresses
Maxi Dresses
Jumpsuits
Short-Sleeve Dresses
Long-Sleeve Dresses
Maxi Skirts

Skirts
Miniskirts
Midi Skirts

Pants
Dress Pants
Cropped Pants

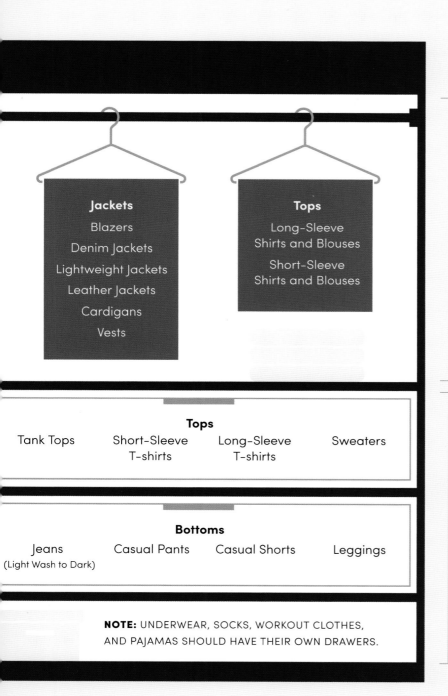

Jackets
Blazers
Denim Jackets
Lightweight Jackets
Leather Jackets
Cardigans
Vests

Tops
Long-Sleeve
Shirts and Blouses
Short-Sleeve
Shirts and Blouses

Tops

| Tank Tops | Short-Sleeve T-shirts | Long-Sleeve T-shirts | Sweaters |

Bottoms

| Jeans (Light Wash to Dark) | Casual Pants | Casual Shorts | Leggings |

NOTE: UNDERWEAR, SOCKS, WORKOUT CLOTHES, AND PAJAMAS SHOULD HAVE THEIR OWN DRAWERS.

Short-Hanging Clothes
Hang short items together, organized by category, so that they don't get lost in long-hanging garments.

Folded Clothes
Fold these items and store them in drawers on a closet shelf. Try to keep each category in its own stack.

Make Lists and Reflect

Before you wrap up the day by treating yourself to a little celebration for getting the job done, jot down these lists while the closet clean-out process is fresh in your mind. Note: You aren't making a complete shopping list here (that comes later!).

WARDROBE GAPS. Are you missing any obvious staples? Do you need to shop for a better version of something that you got rid of?

WARDROBE EXCESSES. What did you have too much of in your closet? What should you avoid buying again (no matter how much you love it), because you have it covered?

OTHER TAKEAWAYS. Did you walk away with any other insights or aha moments?

Congratulations! Take your friend out for a cupcake and celebrate,
because you are officially halfway through your style journey!

WEEK
03

**Style
Awakenings**

Wake Up and Smell the Style

For over a decade I've watched women go through the same vicious cycle of style sabotage: freak out, start a Pinterest board, shop like a madwoman, enjoy a temporary new clothing high, only to freak out a month later when you realize you still have nothing to wear.

Same lame actions. Same lame results. Or, as Tony Robbins puts it: "If you do what you've always done, you'll get what you've always gotten."

It's time to do something different. It's time to get yourself some new and improved results.

Week 3 is devoted to doing things differently. I bet you've never visualized your new sense of style, drafted yourself a dress code, or planned your outfits weeks in advance. This fresh set of actions will bring you closer to the style you crave. Buckle up, sister, because we're only a few weeks away from a brand-new you. Get excited.

Visualize Your Style

Great style rarely comes without a plan.

Years ago I had a conversation with my friend Jane, who owns a home-staging company here in Los Angeles. Jane has a talent for styling homes, but it didn't translate to her wardrobe. Jane had fallen victim to the myth that if you aren't born with personal style then you're SOL.

I decided to give my friend a peek behind the curtain. I showed her how much work goes into getting dressed, not just for my clients but also for myself: the mood boards, the shopping lists, the inspiration, and the goal setting.

I'll never forget it: Jane said, "Dang, girl! You do all this to look good?" Yes, girl, I do. What she didn't realize is that she does the same thing for every other aspect of her life.

Jane doesn't just run to the furniture store to "wing it," buying whatever she likes and hoping it fits and looks good in the room. Before she starts decorating, she creates blueprints, takes measurements, follows a budget, and has a particular aesthetic in mind. My analogy helped Jane jump-start her style plan. After discovering the story she'd been telling herself was completely false, she realized that, as the face of her company, her style was important and worth putting in some effort.

This week you're going to put in some effort too, but I promise you it's going to be fun. No more unpacking emotional baggage, because it's time to pack your bags for the journey ahead. You're going to reflect on your life goals and align them with your style goals.

Draft
Your
Dress
Code

Goal Setting & Style

I'm a goal-setting junkie, for real. Total dork alert, but my annual goal-setting session and vision board–making party is one of the highlights of my year.

Setting goals took me from living off unemployment to making millions, and from style train wreck to a bona fide style expert. The way my life is designed is no accident; I planned and manifested every detail of it.

Today we're going to get clear on your personal and professional goals, then we're going to align them with your personal style. Before we get into the work, I want you to do this fun little visualization exercise. I've taken thousands of women through this process, so you can trust that you're in good hands.

Visualize Your Dream Life

Step 1: Find somewhere quiet and comfortable. No need to get all hippy-dippy with candles and incense. Just find a chill spot with no interruptions.

Step 2: Close your eyes and visualize your perfect life for ten to fifteen minutes. Think about your home, who you're with, your work, your car, your kids, anything. Your dream life has no limits, so have fun with it

Step 3: Open your eyes and look down at what you're wearing, look at your closet, and reflect on your recent outfit choices. Does what you currently wear help get you closer to your dream life?

How did that visualization feel? Did you have any aha moments or did that exercise frustrate the heck out of you? Whatever your reaction was, it's totally fine. This process is designed to shake you up a bit and get you thinking.

Confession Time

For most of my adult life, I swore everyone got the instruction manual but me. Turns out, no one got a manual and we're all just winging it. Goal setting helps me "wing it" with greater accuracy and precision. Add style into the mix and I'm practically unstoppable.

Last year one of my biggest goals was to purchase my first home. It might not sound like a big deal to you, but to me it seemed impossible. Real estate prices in Los Angeles are insane, my savings account was pathetic, and the idea of buying a home without a husband seemed unfathomable. But I put my goal down on paper, visualized living in my home, and made a short and simple action plan:

1. Build up my savings account

2. Set up alerts on Zillow

3. Get an agent and a broker on deck

4. Visit open houses

Now, here is where the style part comes into play. I didn't want to roll into these open houses, banks, and financial institutions in any old outfit. I wanted to show up as a woman who meant business and knew exactly how to close on a house. I knew style was an important piece of the puzzle, based on my prior house-hunting experience.

It was 2010, and my boyfriend and I were finally moving in together. We saw a listing for a great house and decided to pop by on the way to lunch. I happened to have on a Helmut Lang dress with a belly-baring cutout and an Angelina Jolie–style slit. That landlord took one look at me and I knew it was over. We didn't get the house.

Lesson learned. As for my first LA home? I got it. The second house I visited was the one. I dressed the part and signed on the dotted line a month later.

Goal Setting

WHAT ARE YOUR PROFESSIONAL GOALS?

_____

_____

_____

WHAT ARE YOUR PERSONAL GOALS?

_____

_____

_____

WHERE DO YOU SEE YOURSELF:

One year from now?

_____

_____

Five years from now?

_____

_____

Ten years from now?

_____

_____

WHAT MESSAGE DO YOU WANT TO SEND WITH YOUR WARDROBE?

_____

_____

_____

_____

_____

HOW CAN YOUR PRESENT-DAY STYLE CHANGE TO SUPPORT THOSE GOALS?

_____

_____

_____

_____

_____

WHAT ACTIONS CAN YOU TAKE TO SEE THOSE STYLE CHANGES THROUGH? (Purchasing higher-quality garments, eliminating impulse buys, taking more time to get dressed in the morning)

_____

_____

_____

_____

_____

WEEK
3

DAY
15

Virtual Shopping Spree

Isn't it funny how many limitations we put on ourselves? How many unnecessary boxes we create for ourselves? How by default we color inside the lines when we don't have to? We rarely let ourselves play.

Growing up, I was so accustomed to discount shopping, I did it by default as an adult. Most of my money was spent at discount stores, and when I found myself in a full-priced retailer, I only shopped the clearance rack. Because of this limited thinking, I didn't see what was out there, and it hurt the development of my style.

I came up with this fun virtual shopping spree exercise where you shop and "add to cart" completely free of your self-imposed limitations. These limitations could be tied to your finances, your body, the ability to "pull something off," and even your style goals. The purpose of the exercise is to get to the core of your truest sense of style.

You might think this exercise is completely crazy: "What if a neon-green feathered mini dress lands in my cart when my dream is to become a banker?" Don't worry, I'm not going to recommend you buy the dress. Instead you'll interpret the "why" behind the dress choice.

My inspiration for the virtual shopping spree dates back to 2009, when I left my six-figure job and was living off unemployment. My broke behind scraped together ten dollars and bought a book called *The Trick to Money Is Having Some* by Stuart Wilde. It was a game changer. One particular lesson stuck with me: an exercise in abundance that involved going where the money is.

For me it looked like this: Instead of sitting hunched over my laptop at the local coffee shop, I would go work at the lobby bar at the Four Seasons. It costs about the same amount of money for a cup of tea at both places, but the difference in energy was off the charts.

In this luxe environment, I hatched the plan for my personal styling business. There was something about seeing fabulous people come and go (and receiving top-notch service when I ordered just one cup of tea) that inspired me to step up my game. I worked for hours on end. I could smell the success, and I wanted a piece of the action.

Please remember this exercise is meant to be fun and mind-expanding, not stressful. Play. Let your hair down and get crazy. Here's how:

Pick Your Retailer: Head over to an online retailer that sells multiple brands at a higher price point. I recommend Net-a-Porter, but Shopbop, Nordstrom, MyTheresa, and Farfetch are great options too.

Shop Till You Drop: Don't use logic here. When you find something that speaks to you, add it to your cart, or to your wish list if they have that feature. I recommend using the wish list feature, since some shopping carts "expire" and all of your hard work will be lost.

DO NOT Check Out: I'm serious. If you did this exercise right, your cart probably totals $50k plus. No one is going into debt or feeding their secret shopping addiction right now.

Analyze Your Choices: Did you enjoy your shopping spree, or did you overanalyze and talk yourself out of putting things in your cart? As a chronic overanalyzer, I get it. Chances are, one of your roadblocks popped back up. Those suckers are like Whac-A-Mole:

You smack one and moments later it's like, "Hey, girl, I'm over here now." Pay attention to what's going through your head as you do this.

In addition to gaining a ton of style clarity, you may also have some added benefits waiting for you, like:

Manifesting your dream wardrobe. One of my clients really wanted a jacket from her virtual shopping spree. But it was way out of her price range and completely sold out. Cut to a month later. A photo of the jacket appeared on her Pinterest feed, she clicks through, and it takes her to a luxury consignment boutique. What do you know, it's within her budget and in her size! Law of attraction, baby!

Money mindset adjustments. My client Yasmine described the exercises as "liberating." Aligning herself with ease and abundance changed her relationship with money for good.

Reconnecting with old style desires. Sometimes we bury our desires so deep, we forget we even had them! The virtual shopping spree helped my client Stephanie reconnect with herself and her quirky side.

Analyze Your Virtual Shopping Spree

Review your shopping cart or wish list for your virtual shopping spree and answer the following questions:

FEEL IT: How did it feel to shop without limits? Did any of your style roadblocks resurface?

ANALYZE IT: Did you discover any commonalities among your style choices (i.e., did you gravitate toward certain colors, prints, or a particular type of garment)?

NOTE IT: Which styles would you like to add into your real-life wardrobe, if you could find them at affordable prices?

Virtual Shopping Images

Print out images of your favorite pieces from the shopping spree and stick them here.

Find Your Vibe Find Your Vibe Find Your Vibe

Your Style Type

Going shopping for a new wardrobe is a lot like an all-you-can-eat buffet.
Do I want pasta, lobster, a burger, some soft-serve ice cream? How about I have a little bit of each? They're all there for the taking, so there's no need to make a firm culinary decision. But then what happens? Your plate is an absolute mess. Marinara sauce is getting all up in your fish tacos.

The virtual shopping spree was a lot like that buffet. It was a total free-for-all. We pigged out, we released ourselves from the shackles of our style roadblocks, and we finally got to see what appeals to us without those pesky roadblocks in the way.

But let's be clear: We'd *never* shop like that in real life. Gone are the days where you waltz into the mall or click around online picking up whatever strikes your fancy, with zero consideration for your style goals or your style type.

OK, enough fashion. Let's talk about food again. I'm hungry.

I want you to think about going to a regular restaurant. It's up to you to decide what you're in the mood for. Let's say you decide on sushi. Once you get inside the restaurant, the menu is perfectly curated. Not only will you find sushi, you'll find other items that complement that cuisine.

Style types are like that sushi spot. Choosing a style type helps you create definition and guiding principles around what appeals to you and how you want to look, because shopping for your personal style can't and shouldn't be a free-for-all. Identifying your style type is critical to building a wardrobe that works.

I'm about to introduce you to a dozen different style types. They will serve as a great jumping-off point in your journey to refining your unique sense of style. Read through the descriptions below, do some Google image searches of the listed style icons, or check out the Pinterest boards I've created for each style type. I encourage you to find the types you most closely identify with and then use those as inspiration to create your own custom blend.

The Style Types

Polished Professional

Whether your work environment is ultra-conservative or more creative, dressing in a professional manner is key. However, there is always room to insert your personal style. Dressing the part while being true to yourself not only impacts how you're perceived, it helps you show up stronger at the workplace. Trends can be explored and adapted for a business setting as long as the silhouettes are appropriate.

STYLE PERSONA

Assertive
Powerful
Commanding

STYLE ELEMENTS

1. Tailored blazer: for instant polish to a casual look

2. Pointed pumps and a structured bag: the best quality you can afford

3. Classic tops like a button-down blouse, crewneck cashmere sweater

STYLE ICONS

- Alexandria Ocasio-Cortez
- Cameron Diaz in The Other Woman
- Gavyn Taylor (@gavyntaylor)+
- Ivanka Trump
- Katrina Lake
- Kerry Washington in Scandal
- Lauren Nicole (@laurennicolefk)+
- May Musk *
- Meghan Markle in Suits
- Melora Hardin in The Bold Type*
- Meryl Streep in The Devil Wears Prada
- Michelle Obama*
- Oprah*
- Queen Rania of Jordan
- Robin Wright in House of Cards*
- Viola Davis in How to Get Away with Murder*

Tastefully Timeless

The Tastefully Timeless style type is just that: timeless. Take a photo of her, and you wouldn't be able to tell if it was taken in 1920 or 2020. With a wardrobe built using classics that can be mixed and matched to create endless looks, this style type always remains fresh.

STYLE PERSONA

Classic
Refined
Sophisticated

STYLE ELEMENTS

1. Classic trench coat: perfect for layering in spring and autumn

2. Glen plaid blazer: this timeless print never goes out of style

3. Hermes scarf: or any silk scarf with equestrian-inspired design

STYLE ICONS

- Ali MacGraw in Love Story
- Amal Clooney
- Anna Wintour
- Audrey Hepburn in Breakfast at Tiffany's
- Brooke Shields*
- Carmon Dell'Orefice *
- Carolina Herrera*
- Charlize Theron
- Coco Chanel
- Emmanuelle Alt
- Faye Dunaway in Bonnie and Clyde
- Françoise Hardy
- Grace Kelly
- Jacqueline Kennedy Onassis
- Jean Seberg in Breathless
- Kate Middleton
- Mary Lambert+
- Nicolette Mason (@nicholettemason)+

* = OVER-50 ICON   + = PLUS-SIZE ICON

The Style Types (*cont.*)

The Minimalist

Not to be confused with the minimalist movement/capsule collections where the less in your closet is more, the minimalist style harkens back to the 1990s Calvin Klein days with clean lines, simple shapes, and a neutral color palette.

STYLE PERSONA

Bold
Austere
No-Fuss

STYLE ELEMENTS

1. Silk slip dress: for a clean and simple evening ready look

2. Black or white pantsuit: limited colors for maximum impact

3. Cut out and strong shoulder tops: give visual interest without loud prints

STYLE ICONS

- Angelina Jolie
- Carole Bouquet*
- Carolyn Bessette Kennedy
- Cate Blanchett*
- Clémence Poésy
- Diane Keaton*
- Elin Kling
- Hanneli Mustaparta
- Iman*
- Isabelle Decker (@dressingoutsidethebox) +
- Monica Vitti
- Kris Jenner *
- Phoebe Philo
- Rochelle Johnson (@iambeauticurve) +
- Sofia Coppola
- Tilda Swinton*
- Tonne Goodman*
- Vera Wang
- Winona Ryder
- Yoko Ono *

Perfectly Preppy

The preppy look has come a long way since the popped collars of the 1980s. The Perfectly Preppy style type is playful, a bit demure, and likes to have a little fun with fashion. Classic silhouettes in bold colors with a touch of whimsy best describe this look.

STYLE PERSONA

Whimsical Energetic Fun

STYLE ELEMENTS

1. Denim jacket: versatile layer to dress down any look

2. Pair of loafers: preppy, comfy, and so chic

3. Plaid: to tap into your inner Cher (from *Clueless*, duh)

STYLE ICONS

- Aidy Bryant in <u>Shrill</u> +
- Alexa Chung
- Alicia Silverstone in <u>Clueless</u>
- Anna Kendrick
- Anne Hathaway
- Beanie Feldstein in <u>Booksmart</u> +
- Blair Eadie
- Carey Mulligan in <u>An Education</u>
- Helen Mirren*
- Jenna Lyons
- Julie Andrews in <u>The Princess Diaries</u> *
- Kate Spade
- Lilly Pulitzer
- Leighton Meester in <u>Gossip Girl</u>
- Millie Bobby Brown
- Princess Diana
- Reese Witherspoon
- Taylor Swift
- The cast of <u>Heathers</u>

* = OVER-50 ICON   + = PLUS-SIZE ICON

The Style Types *(cont.)*

Casual Chic

For those after comfort and style, the Casual Chic style type is the perfect starting point. Casual Chic plays with all of the wardrobe staples we love (denim, T-shirts, and cozy knits) but arranges them in a way that screams polished. This style type is relaxed, laid-back, and most important, comfortable.

STYLE PERSONA

Easygoing
Understated
Laid-back

STYLE ELEMENTS

1. Jeans in a variety of silhouettes (boyfriend, straight-leg, skinny)

2. Stylish sneakers: go classic with Converse or trendy with Golden Goose

3. Striped tee: give those plain tees a break

STYLE ICONS

- Amber Riley+
- Cameron Diaz
- Candice Kelly (@candicekellyxo)+
- Gabi Fresh (@gabifresh)+
- Heidi Klum
- Hilary Duff
- Jane Fonda*
- Jennifer Aniston
- Jessica Alba
- Jessica Biel
- Katie Holmes
- Louise Roe (@louiseroe)
- Mila Kunis
- Pamela Adlon*
- Sandra Bullock *

Street-Style Chic

Women who gravitate toward Street-Style Chic typically enjoy taking risks (or actively striving to take bigger risks in life). They are always game for re-creating themselves through bold style choices. Trends don't scare this style type at all, and they are willing to experiment.

STYLE PERSONA

Adventurous Flamboyant Showy

STYLE ELEMENTS

1. Logo mania: show off your designer love with strategically placed logos

2. Mixed prints: mixing stripes and leopard is always a fun combo

3. Runway styles: because only you can truly pull them off!

STYLE ICONS

- Anna Dello Russo
- Chiara Ferragni
- Chriselle Lim
- Eva Chen
- Giovanna Battaglia
- Hailey Rhode Bieber
- Leandra Medine
- Jazzmyne Robbins (@jazzmynejay)*
- Kendall Jenner
- Miroslava Duma
- Nicolette Mason+
- Olivia Palermo
- Patti Gibbons (@notdeadyetstyle)*
- Rihanna
- Sarah Jane Adams (@saramaijewels)*
- Sarah Jessica Parker in Sex and the City
- Tess Holliday+

* = OVER-50 ICON   + = PLUS-SIZE ICON

The Style Types *(cont.)*

Tomboy Style

When it comes to influences, the Tomboy style type borrows from the boys. Baggier silhouettes, masculine elements (like blazers and trousers), and strategically placed street wear, and the overall vibe of carefree comfort play a huge role in this particular look.

STYLE PERSONA

Sporty
Gamine
Relaxed

STYLE ELEMENTS

1. Sporty sneakers: the latest releases from Adidas and Nike. Sneakerheads, this is your moment!

2. Hoodies: paired with something unexpected like tuxedo trousers or a flirty skirt

3. Graphic tees: modern or vintage are both great options

STYLE ICONS

- Agyness Deyn
- Alison Mosshart
- Amel Bent
- Cara Delevingne
- Diane Keaton in Annie Hall
- Ellen Degeneres*
- Ellen Page
- Freja Beha Erichsen
- Janelle Monáe
- Katharine Hepburn
- Kristen Stewart
- Lauren Bacall
- Lauren Hutton*
- Linda Rodin*
- Marlene Dietrich
- Queen Latifah+

Edgy Classic

Dark, mysterious, and often a bit dangerous best describes the woman who identifies with the Edgy Classic style type. If this style type had an astrological sign, it would be a Scorpio. The garments that fall into the Edgy Classic camp have a darker color palette (black is a go-to, with pops of reds) and daring details like zippers, studs, leather, and lace.

STYLE PERSONA

Fearless
Daring
Strong

STYLE ELEMENTS

1. Leather motorcycle jacket: easy to dress up or dress down

2. Vintage concert tees: an edgy girl staple

3. Black: when in doubt, wear black

STYLE ICONS

- Beth Ditto+
- Barbie Ferreira +
- Carine Roitfeld*
- Chrissy Teigen
- Christine Centenera
- Daphne Guinness*
- Elle King+
- Emily Ratajkowski
- Gwen Stefani
- Inès de la Fressange*
- Lyn Slater*
- Miranda Kerr
- Micah Gianneli
- Rooney Mara
- Rebel Wilson+
- Rosie Huntington–Whiteley

* = OVER-50 ICON   + = PLUS-SIZE ICON

The Style Types (*cont.*)

Subtle Sexy

This style type is often tapped into for date night or social events, but for some, inserting a little sexy into everyday attire is the perfect way to celebrate femininity and have some fun. Curve-hugging silhouettes, peekaboo elements, and the strategic showing of body parts are key for this style type.

STYLE PERSONA

Seductive Alluring Sultry

STYLE ELEMENTS

1. Bodycon dress: to show off those killer curves

2. Pencil skirts: wear them to work or for date night

3. Silk, satin, and lace: bedroom-appropriate fabrics translate as sexy in your daily wardrobe

STYLE ICONS

- Adele+
- Angela Bassett*
- Anne Bancroft in The Graduate
- Ashley Graham+
- Blake Lively
- Christina Hendricks
- Cher*
- Dita Von Teese
- Eva Mendes
- Halle Berry*
- Jennifer Lopez*
- Kim Kardashian
- Lizzo+
- Meghan Trainor+
- Penélope Cruz
- Scarlett Johansson

Modern Romantic

"Feminine," "soft," and "whimsical" would all be great words to describe this style type. The Modern Romantic leans into her femininity and is completely unapologetic about it. Pastel colors, lace, ruffles, and flirty silhouettes (fit-and-flare Peter Pan collars) are all hallmarks of this look.

STYLE PERSONA

Soft
Feminine
Modest

STYLE ELEMENTS

1. Floral prints: bring in some botanicals to instantly soften your look

2. Pussy bow blouses: pair perfectly with both skirts and jeans

3. Pastels: try a pastel pantsuit or keep is classic with fit and flare dress

STYLE ICONS

- Lauren Conrad
- Zooey Deschanel
- Dakota Fanning
- Diane Kruger
- Emma Stone
- Melissa McCarthy+
- Poppy Delevingne
- Chanel Iman
- Chrissy Metz+
- Musician Alison Sudol
- Saoirse Ronan
- Greta Gerwig
- Keira Knightley
- Emmy Rossum
- Kristin Chirico+
- Grece Ghanem*
- Faye Dunaway*
- Molly Ringwald*

* = OVER-50 ICON   + = PLUS-SIZE ICON

Upgraded Bohemian

The Upgraded Bohemian is free-spirited and connected to nature but isn't one to turn away a great pair of designer shoes given the opportunity—know what I'm saying? This style type is inspired by the elements, and loves the styles from the sixties and seventies (maxi skirts, paisley prints, suede, fringe, and layered jewelry).

STYLE PERSONA

Carefree
Free spirit
Nonconformist

STYLE ELEMENTS

1. Vintage kimono or duster over a jeans and a tee shirt for instant cool

2. Suede, earth tones, and fringe: take it all the way back to the '60s and '70s

3. Layered necklaces and stacked bracelets (mixing chains, beads, and crystals)

STYLE ICONS

- Anita Pallenberg
- Florence Welch
- Georgia May Jagger
- Jane Birkin
- Julie Henderson (@juliehenderson32)+
- Kate Moss
- Kate Bosworth
- Marianne Faithfull
- Mary-Kate Olsen
- Nicole Richie
- Pat Cleveland*
- Rachel Zoe
- Sheryl Crow*
- Sienna Miller
- Vanessa Hudgens
- Zoë Kravitz

Eclectic Warrior

Not be confused with a style chameleon who changes her style every time the wind blows (Madonna would be an excellent example of this), the Eclectic Warrior layers a multitude of styles to create her own specific look. Think art teacher meets the runway—unique and fashion forward without being trendy.

STYLE PERSONA

Worldly
Multifaceted
Quirky

STYLE ICONS

- Chloë Sevigny
- Danielle Brooks+
- Diane Von Furstenberg*
- Diana Vreeland
- Iris Apfel*
- Julia Sarr-Jamois
- Lupita Nyong'o
- Melanie Kobayashi*
- Prue Leith*
- Sofia Boutella
- Solange Knowles
- Tracee Ellis Ross
- Virgie Tovar (@virgietovar)+
- Yara Shahidi
- Zendaya

STYLE ELEMENTS

1. Vintage: explore treasures from different time periods and make them your own

2. Ethnic pieces: pick up jewelry, clothing, and accessories during international travel

3. Prints: when in doubt, choose the print!

* = OVER-50 ICON   + = PLUS-SIZE ICON

Create Your Custom Style Type

Use Pinterest to create a board with your favorite looks and then build out your style type. You can start by re-pinning images that you like from my Pinterest Style Type boards and then add your favorite style icons, designers, and television and movie characters. Try specific searches for clothing that you need like "stylish suits" or "sneakers with dresses." Then take a step back and answer these questions.

IDENTIFY IT: Which style types appeal the most to you? If your style type had a name, what would it be?

_____

_____

_____

_____

DESCRIBE IT: What does your style type say about you?

_____

_____

_____

_____

_____

_____

_____

_____

BREAK IT DOWN: What are the most important elements of your custom style type (i.e., contrasting patterns, structure and tailoring, feminine details, or flowy garments)?

PICK YOUR PALETTE: What colors will you stick with?

Your Dream Life(style)

When I was twenty-five years old, I got hired for a job I was underqualified for. The CEO interviewed me for the position. I tried my best to BS my way through his questions, but I was drowning. At the time, I knew nothing about tech or building an online community (look at me now, suckers). However, I did have one quality he was looking for: I had a vision.

The CEO asked me which techniques I used to plan for the future. That was one of the few questions I had an answer to. I created vision boards. I had been making vision boards since I was twenty years old, and the majority of the time whatever I stuck on those boards became my reality.

After leaving that job to become a full-time stylist, I started creating vision boards with my style in mind. The results were mind-blowing. I found that visualizing myself all dressed for my future helped me achieve my goals faster.

I want you to do the same thing right now. Create two vision boards, one for your life and one for your style. Start by gathering images that represent the life you'd like to have. Images of your dream house, loved ones, travel destinations, projects you want to complete, awards or achievements, important mantras, and other goals. These images will make up your lifestyle board. Next, you'll print out key images from your style type research (your favorite pieces and icons). These will go on your style board.

Even if you consider yourself to be the un-craftiest girl on the block, please trust me and make at least one collage. If you are as gung-ho about making vision boards as I am, feel free to fill the next three blank pages.

Your Vision Boards Here!

Your Vision Boards Here!

Draft Your Dress Code

Isn't it a bummer when you land your dream job only to discover there's a dress code? Or even worse, you land the opposite of your dream job and have to wear a uniform? The horror. Where's the freedom? How will you express yourself? And for those of us who don't have to follow a dress code or wear a uniform, don't you wish (just a little bit) that you did? It's one less decision to make in a day.

What if I told you that you could have your creative freedom *and* the structure a uniform provides? You can have both of those things in what I call a Style Uniform. A Style Uniform is a go-to outfit combination that is unique to you. It's flattering, it falls within your style type, and it suits your lifestyle.

Let's use myself as an example. I'm a SoCal-based entrepreneur who works in fashion. I need to be comfortable, casual, and fashion forward in business settings. If I were to book a last-minute meeting or an appearance and didn't want to spend hours agonizing over what to wear, I'd turn to my Style Uniform. My professional Style Uniform is a pair of jeans, a fun jacket or blazer, a T-shirt, and statement heels. I can re-create and shop around this one uniform a million times over.

Note the word "shop." You do not need a closet full of clothes to create your Style Uniform. The only thing you need is a vision.

I created a worksheet to help guide you through the process of creating your Style Uniform. Fill it out and then start experimenting. If you don't nail it the first time, that's OK; try again until you find what works for you. Trust me, once you figure this out, shopping and getting dressed are going to be so much easier.

I should mention that having more than one uniform is OK and encouraged. Your professional Style Uniform may be different from your weekend uniform. For example, I'm not stomping around the dog park in a fun blazer and heals. My weekend uniform is more relaxed; jeans, T-shirt, leather jacket, and stylish sneakers.

To create a Style Uniform, you need to filter your style type (your vibe) through the lens of these practical considerations:

Routine and lifestyle. Do you need sensible shoes for your commute? The right layers for your chilly office? Do you need outfits for client meetings and interviews? What about cocktail parties and brunches?

Physical comfort. Are you always too cold? Or do you sweat easily? Which fabrics are you happiest in (and are there any that irritate you)? Do you have foot problems that limit your shoe options?

Body confidence. Are you clear on which garments flatter your figure? And on which silhouettes you can wear with confidence? Flip to pages 184–185 in the reference section for some pointers on this.

Time for maintenance. Can you put the time into ironing, hand-washing, or dry-cleaning your clothes, or is it more realistic to have a wardrobe of machine-washable garments? If you're unsure of how to care for something, check out my fabric maintenance guide on pages 190–191.

Your Style Uniform (Professional)

NAME:	AGE:	TITLE:
Kara	46	CEO, public relations agency

STYLE TYPE:	3 WORDS:
Polished Professional	Powerful, Successful, Driven

DESCRIPTION:

Founded a New York – based, female – run public relations agency ten years ago. Serves as the face of the company. Regularly speaks on panels and spends a considerable amount of time on the road.

SCENARIO:

Early flight from NYC to Austin, with a presentation in the afternoon.

Professional Style Uniform

CLOTHES:

Cigarette Pants + Boxy Blazer + Silk Blouse

ACCESSORIES:

Leopard Print Pumps + Structured Tote + Gold Cuff Bracelet

Your Style Uniform (Professional)

DESCRIBE YOUR WORK LIFE. Include your office dress code; job functions, like presentations and client meetings; environmental factors (i.e., stuffy conference rooms); and your commute.

_____

_____

_____

_____

_____

STYLE IT: Now create one style uniform for an important work scenario.

Professional Uniform

SCENARIO:

_____

_____

CLOTHING:

_____

_____

SHOES:

_____

ACCESSORIES:

_____

JEWELRY:

_____

WEEK
3

DAY
19

Your Style Uniform (Social)

NAME:	AGE:	TITLE:
Shana	27	Freelance television writer

STYLE TYPE:	3 WORDS:
Upgraded Bohemian	Creative, Fun, Smart

DESCRIPTION:

Recently moved from Ohio to Los Angeles. Works all day, networks all night in an effort to advance in her career — and for the free food and drinks! Working with a limited budget, but also has to leave lasting impressions.

SCENARIO:

Happy hour with friends in the industry.

Social Style Uniform

CLOTHES:

Little Black Dress + Kimono (or Duster)

ACCESSORIES:

Statement Sandals + Wristlet Evening Bag + Layered Delicate Jewelry

Your Style Uniform (Social)

DESCRIBE YOUR SOCIAL LIFE. This includes date nights or dating, cocktail parties, hanging out with friends, taking classes, or going to music festivals.

_____

_____

_____

_____

_____

STYLE IT: Now create one style uniform that addresses an important part of your social life.

Social Uniform

SCENARIO:

_____

_____

CLOTHING:

_____

_____

SHOES:

_____

ACCESSORIES:

_____

JEWELRY:

_____

WEEK
3

DAY
19

Your Style Uniform (Weekend)

CLIENT EXAMPLE

NAME:	AGE:	TITLE:
Jennifer	30	Blogger and Stay-at-Home Mom

STYLE TYPE:	3 WORDS:
Casual Chic	Responsible, Nurturing, Youthful

DESCRIPTION:

Lives in a suburb outside of Washington, D.C. Spends the day working from home while her two young kids are at school. Weekends are devoted to soccer games, birthday parties, and fun excursions (museums, movies). Comfort is key.

SCENARIO:

Typical Saturday of soccer, lunch with the family, and a trip to the movies

Weekend Style Uniform

CLOTHES:

Maxi Dress + Denim Jacket

ACCESSORIES:

Stylish Sneakers + Cross-Body Bag + Sunglasses + Statement Earrings

Your Style Uniform (Social)

DESCRIBE HOW YOU SPEND YOUR DOWNTIME. This might entail gardening or exercising, snuggling on the couch and watching TV, or doing craft projects.

_____

_____

_____

_____

_____

STYLE IT: Now create one style uniform that addresses your favorite downtime scenario.

Weekend Uniform

SCENARIO:

_____

CLOTHING:

_____

SHOES:

_____

ACCESSORIES:

_____

JEWELRY:

_____

WEEK
3

DAY
19

Closet Quickie

You've already cleaned out your closet, but my guess is there are probably some stragglers that could stand to exit stage right. I'm talking about the pieces you knew weren't great, but they weren't terrible enough to toss.

Since it's Day 20, and you have some additional clarity on your side, it's time to reassess what's hanging in your closet. It's kind of like running back inside to make sure you unplugged the curling iron before leaving for the office. You know you unplugged it, but *maybe* you didn't, so you check again. And please don't tell me I'm the only one who does this!

It's time for a double-check, my friend, aka a closet cleanse quickie. I want you to head back into your closet for one last wardrobe review before you create your shopping list.

Before you create your shopping list, ask yourself these questions for the remaining items hanging in your closet.

- Does this garment support my vision (for my life and style)?

- Can this garment be restyled to align with my vision and new style type?

If you're still undecided if a garment should stay or go? Place it in what I call a "Maybe Box." A Maybe Box is like purgatory for your clothes. If you find yourself saying, "Maybe this will fit someday" or "Maybe this will come back in style," in the box it goes!

Make a note on your calendar to revisit the box in a few months. If you genuinely missed something, feel free to place it back in your closet. If you didn't miss it, that's a clear sign that it's time to donate or consign.

Closet Quickie

Stand in front of your (beautifully organized—see Day 14) closet and do a rough assessment.

Current Closet

Divide this circle to represent the percentage of your wardrobe that is devoted to work, weekend, and socializing.

Goal Closet

Now adjust your percentages of clothes devoted to work, weekend, and socializing so that your wardrobe more accurately reflects the various parts of your life.

WEEK
3

DAY
20

Create Your Shopping List

There are two types of terrible shoppers:

1. Those who hate shopping. They avoid shopping at all costs, and it shows through their dated wardrobe.

2. Those who love to shop but use it as an escape. The escape artist shopper shops to fill a void and often overspends.

What we're aiming for is something right in between, where shopping is enjoyable but, most important, productive.

Growing up, I couldn't stand shopping; my mom would drag me around town while she ran a zillion and a half errands. The highlight of our shopping trips was at the end of the day when I got to pick out a fresh pair of jelly shoes at Kmart.

I wasn't raised to shop with a list. Instead we just shopped till we dropped. I was a kid, so I didn't see anything wrong with this type of shopping, but as an adult the problem is glaring. When you shop without a list, you're almost guaranteed to overspend and stress yourself out. Don't do it! I would never shop for a client without a list, and you shouldn't either.

Take a look at your Ultimate Wardrobe Checklist; the highlighted items—the items you don't yet own *and* that align with the vision for your new sense of style—will go on the "Basics" shopping list (page 132).

Next, review your Style Vision Board and Style Uniform worksheets and decide which items you'd like to purchase to craft your signature style. Those items will go on your "Signature Style" shopping list (page 133).

Let's give credit where it's due, and the credit goes straight to you! You've done a ton of work to get to this point. Let's pull all your style insights onto one happy little page. I recommend snapping a picture of these pages so you have them handy during your next shopping excursions.

Build Your Shopping List

YOUR STYLE TYPE:

_____

YOUR COLOR PALETTE:

☐ ☐ ☐ ☐ ☐

Work Your three words for your work style (see page x)

1. _____   **2.** _____   **3.** _____

Key basics and signature pieces for work:

_____

_____

Social Life Your three words for your social style (see page x)

1. _____   **2.** _____   **3.** _____

Key basics and signature pieces for your social life:

_____

_____

Weekend Your three words for your weekend style (see page x)

1. _____   **2.** _____   **3.** _____

Key basics and signature pieces for the weekend:

_____

_____

WEEK
3

DAY
21

Build Your Shopping List (Basics)

ITEM	PRIORITY		
	LOW	MED	HIGH
	LOW	MED	HIGH
	LOW	MED	HIGH
	LOW	MED	HIGH
	LOW	MED	HIGH
	LOW	MED	HIGH
	LOW	MED	HIGH
	LOW	MED	HIGH
	LOW	MED	HIGH
	LOW	MED	HIGH
	LOW	MED	HIGH
	LOW	MED	HIGH
	LOW	MED	HIGH
	LOW	MED	HIGH
	LOW	MED	HIGH
	LOW	MED	HIGH

Build Your Shopping List (Signature Style)

ITEM	PRIORITY
	LOW MED HIGH
	LOW MED HIGH
	LOW MED HIGH
	LOW MED HIGH
	LOW MED HIGH
	LOW MED HIGH
	LOW MED HIGH
	LOW MED HIGH
	LOW MED HIGH
	LOW MED HIGH
	LOW MED HIGH
	LOW MED HIGH
	LOW MED HIGH
	LOW MED HIGH
	LOW MED HIGH
	LOW MED HIGH

WEEK
3

DAY
21

WEEK
04

Your Signature Style

Time to Reveal Your Signature Style

There comes a time in every woman's life when following the trends and buying whatever the "cool kids" are wearing gets old.

I mean, who wants to be that one chick from Mean Girls who said, "I saw Cady Heron wearing army pants and flip-flops. So I bought army pants and flip-flops."

When you're a strong, independent woman like yourself, being a follower just doesn't fit. You don't look like yourself, you don't feel like yourself, plus all of that follower-mentality shopping gets expensive.

During this final week of your style transformation, you are going to put everything you've learned about yourself and your style to the test. This is the SAT of style, my friend. You're going to shop, you're going to put together outfits, and you're going to walk away from this experience with a sense of style that you can call your own.

In Week 1, the 7-Day Selfie Challenge captured your "before." Now it's time to reveal your "after."

WEEK
4

Style in Action

Shopping for a living? Sign me up. That's exactly what went through my head when I started my career as a personal stylist. Little did I know, the way a stylist shops is much different from how the average woman shops.

I was accustomed to living my best life at the mall. You know, aimlessly perusing the racks, trying things on, buying pieces here and there. I rarely thought about how the garments I was purchasing would work with the rest of my wardrobe. Nor did I consider what my new wardrobe would do to improve the quality of my life.

It wasn't until I started shopping for clients that things began to click. I couldn't take my sweet time curating my clients' wardrobes. For each client, I had less than two days to build an entire wardrobe. Shopping that way requires some serious strategy and a full-on game plan.

The strategies I put in place also needed to go beyond shopping. I had to consider what would happen <u>after</u> I shopped: styling the look and how to get those finishing touches just right—I'm talking shoes, jewelry, and accessories. I needed to shop with speed and with the "after" in mind.

Once I mastered these shopping strategies, everything changed. I was able to help my clients shop in record time and without the stress. The strategies you're going to learn this week are pro-level. If you do what I've outlined, it's game over, baby! You will be walking around looking like a million and a half bucks, I guarantee it.

Let's Do Some Shopping!

Shop Like a Stylist

I'll never forget my first time shopping as a stylist. I was assisting a celebrity stylist prep for a music video. We had one day to shop for the lead singer, the band, and the backup singers. I was tasked with hitting fifteen stores in one day. Here's what I learned from that experience, and how it applies to the intensive shopping you're about to do.

How to Shop Like a Stylist

MAKE A PLAN

Depending on your stamina and how much you need to buy, you'll very likely need more than a day to shop. Pace yourself, but try to stay on task so you don't lose momentum. Give yourself a deadline for completing this part of your journey, because the real styling begins once you actually have the goods in hand!

Before you start shopping, create a list of stores you'd like to visit (see pages 142–143 for suggestions by Style Type) and establish a budget. Bring your shopping list and your inspiration with you. Pop your vision boards into your purse or make the digital files easily accessible on your phone.

DO A PULL

Stylists don't go shopping; they call it doing a "pull." Pulling clothes means hitting a list of stores that fit the desired aesthetic and your budget. A stylist will grab whatever catches their eye, bring it back to the studio, create looks, and return what doesn't work.

I found this method of shopping to be absolutely genius; it's much more efficient than agonizing over every piece you pick up and cobbling together complete outfits inside the store. I started shopping this way for my own wardrobe, and then began teaching my virtual clients the same methodology. It means plunking down some major money and then doing returns,* so keep your receipts organized and don't remove any tags (more on that later)!

Always ask for the store's return policy before making a purchase.

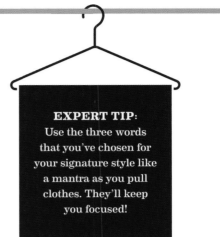

EXPERT TIP:
Use the three words
that you've chosen for
your signature style like
a mantra as you pull
clothes. They'll keep
you focused!

STICK TO YOUR GOALS

While I encourage you to pull more clothes than you'll ultimately keep, you are still shopping with intention. Don't let the salespeople be your stylist. You know what you're doing this time. Check in with yourself as you select garments by asking the following questions:

- Why am I buying this?

- What is my emotional state right now?

- Do I think buying this will give me a quick fix emotionally?

- Do I have something like this in my closet already?

- Can I create at least three outfits with it?

- Can I afford to purchase it?

- Can I resell it or consign it later?

IN STORE OR ONLINE?

While I do love shopping online, that doesn't mean 100 percent of my wardrobe comes from online retailers. Doing some in-store shopping could be more efficient because you can react firsthand to the garments (no reading reviews, taking a gamble on the color or quality, and waiting for the package to arrive). However, whether you shop online or in-store, your final purchasing decision happens at home.

So what does that mean? It means everything you purchase isn't officially added to your wardrobe until you put on an at-home fashion show. When your shopping spree is complete, turn to Day 23 (page 144) for the most fun part of the process yet!

WEEK
4

DAY
22

Go Shopping

It's time to hit the stores! I've listed a few of my favorite stores and brands categorized by style type. Do you have to shop these exact stores and brands? Absolutely not. Look them up on online to get a feel for the merchandise, but shop wherever you feel the most comfortable and confident.

Stores and Brands by Style Type

POLISHED PROFESSIONAL

- L'Agence
- Theory
- Vince
- Equipment
- Veronica Beard

TASTEFULLY TIMELESS

- Banana Republic
- Sandro
- Everlane
- Ralph Lauren
- Brooks Brothers

THE MINIMALIST

- COS
- Tibi
- Mansur Gavriel
- Rachel Comey
- AYR

PERFECTLY PREPPY

- J.Crew
- Alice + Olivia
- Kate Spade
- Lilly Pulitzer
- Tommy Hilfiger

CASUAL CHIC

- Madewell
- ASOS
- Frame
- Shopbop
- Target

STREET-STYLE CHIC

- Kirna Zabête
- Intermix
- Curvy Sense
- Zara
- H&M

TOMBOY STYLE

- Adidas
- Rag & Bone
- One DNA
- VEEA
- Acne Studios

EDGY CLASSIC

- AllSaints
- SSENSE
- Helmut Lang
- The Kooples
- Alexander Wang

SUBTLE SEXY

- BCBG
- Revolve
- Cushnie
- Fame & Partners
- Michelle Mason

EXPERT TIP: Avoid online retailers with rock-bottom prices. Often the clothing pictured is not what you're getting in the mail. With turtle-slow shipping and bad return polices, it's best to just say no.

EXPERT TIP: Look to high-end designers for style inspiration. Going straight to the source will elevate your taste so that you're prepped to spot a comparable look for less.

MODERN ROMANTIC
- A.L.C.
- Maje
- Coach
- Alexis
- Alice McCall

UPGRADED BOHEMIAN
- Free People
- Anthropologie
- Johnny Was
- Zimmerman
- Isabel Marant

ECLECTIC WARRIOR
- Vintage boutiques
- Thrift shops
- Opening Ceremony
- Marni
- Dries Van Noten

SHOPPING FOR ALL TYPES
- Farfetch
- Moda Operandi
- Neiman Marcus
- Net-a-Porter
- Nordstrom
- Saks Fifth Avenue

ECO-FRIENDLY SHOPPING
- Maison de Mode
- Ethica
- Amour Vert
- Hazel & Rose
- Rêve En Vert

WEEK
4

DAY
22

OTHERS TO CHECK OUT

Your At-Home Fashion Show

Fitting rooms are the worst! Am I right? The lighting, the mirrors, and the pushy sales associates all put a damper on the buying experience. Why subject yourself to that fluorescent nightmare when you don't have to? It's time to level up your try-on experience, and it all happens in the comfort of your home. Here's how.

Trying It All On

STEP 1:

Make it fun.

Fitting rooms are one of the most un-fun places on earth, but your home? Oh yeah, we've got some real fun potential there! Create an environment that psyches you up: crank some tunes, pop some popcorn (just don't get butter on the clothes), or pour yourself a cup of tea. Do whatever it takes to make trying on clothes a positive experience.

STEP 2:

Pull everything out.

It's time to see your new purchases without the bad lighting and mirrors. Not only that, when you're at home, you get to try things on with your other clothes, shoes, and accessories. And be sure to ask yourself the following questions during the try-on process:

- Do I love this?

- Does this fit me?

- Can it be altered to fit?

- What will I wear with this?

- Where will I wear this?

- Can I walk and sit comfortably in this?

- Are the washing and care instructions practical for me?

EXPERT TIP:
Be mindful of your makeup. There is a chance some of these items will be returned, so avoid wearing foundation and bright-colored lipstick.

EXPERT TIP:
Get a tagging gun. Tagging guns are cheap (you can find them on Amazon) and are great for reattaching fallen tags during the try-on process.

STEP 3:

Get an opinion.

When you're at home, you can get a much-needed second opinion from a friend, spouse, or even social media. In the store, your second opinion (the sales associate) has ulterior motives and you really don't need that tainted point of view in your life right now.

STEP 4:

Snap some selfies.

If there's no one around to weigh in, take a selfie. Sometimes seeing your purchase in a photo makes a world of difference. As it turns out, those cute black pants are actually green and somehow completely sheer.

STEP 5.

Don't pop the tags!

Today you are trying on your purchases primarily to see what fits and feels good. Do not remove any tags! Over the next few days, you'll revisit your purchases with an eye toward outfit building (and you'll also see whether a garment still has the magic 72 hours later).

WEEK

4

DAY

23

Log Your Haul

Use this page to log in your purchases so that you can keep track of what you spent and whether you plan to keep, alter, exchange, or return each item.

ITEM	COST	KEEP/RETURN/EXCHANGE/ALTER
	$	
	$	
	$	
	$	
	$	
	$	
	$	
	$	
	$	
	$	
	$	
	$	
	$	
	$	
	$	

ITEM	COST	KEEP/RETURN/EXCHANGE/ALTER
	$	
	$	
	$	
	$	
	$	
	$	
	$	
	$	
	$	
	$	
	$	
	$	
	$	
	$	
	$	
	$	
	$	
	$	

WEEK
4

DAY
23

Easy Outfit Formulas

On Day 19 you created your Style Uniform, a go-to outfit combination that speaks to your personal style and lifestyle. If you recall, mine consisted of jeans, a fun blazer, a T-shirt, and heels. As much as I love that getup, the world would be a very boring place if I wore that outfit combination every single day. Since variety is the spice of life, it's time we start shaking things up a bit.

By now you've got yourself some new clothes and a fresh new attitude centered around your new sense of style, which means you are ready to expand your outfit horizons. That's right: It's time to start incorporating some Outfit Formulas into your routine. Don't let the word "formula" intimidate you; there is zero math involved. These formulas are designed to jump-start your creativity and get you out of your outfit comfort zone.

Look back at the images on your mood board and dissect your favorite looks. A formula could be "Slouchy Sweater + Mini Dress + Booties" or "Kimono + Boyfriend Jeans + Graphic Tee + Loafers." Getting as many formulas down as you can; this makes outfit creation a breeze.

I've created fifteen different formulas for you to experiment with. Use your new clothes, use your old clothes, and don't freak out if you don't own one of the items on the formula list. Do what you can and make substitutions if you get stumped.

Remember that I suggested waiting before you rip off tags and toss out your receipts? That's because I want you to put your new purchases to the test, to see how many different outfits these pieces generate. The final decision about what stays and what goes back comes *after* this exercise.

Easy Outfit Formulas: Work

FORMULA #1:

Statement Blazer + Bodysuit + Trouser + Booties

FORMULA #2:

Pantsuit + Silk Blouse + Statement Necklace + Pumps

FORMULA #3:

Pencil Skirt + Fitted Sweater + Silk Scarf + Pumps

FORMULA #4:

Pussy Bow Blouse + Blazer + Wide-Leg Pants + Stacked Heels

FORMULA #5:

Power Dress + Pumps + Blazer + Statement Necklace

Easy Outfit Formulas: Social

FORMULA #1:
Leather Jacket + Jeans + Graphic Tee + Pumps

FORMULA #2:
Camisole + Blazer + Leather Leggings + Boots

FORMULA #3:
Little Black Dress + Duster + Strappy Sandals + Clutch

FORMULA #4:
Crop Top + High Waist Pants + Blazer + Pumps

FORMULA #5:
Silk Blouse + Lace Bralette + Leather Pants + Booties

Easy Outfit Formulas: Weekend

FORMULA #1:
Shirtdress + Waist-cinching belt + Cardigan + Sandals

FORMULA #2:
Joggers + Striped Tee + Leather Jacket + Sneakers

FORMULA #3:
Chambray Top + Jeans + Trench Coat + Loafers

FORMULA #4:
Maxi Dress + Denim Jacket + Sneakers + Statement Necklace

FORMULA #5:
Tee Shirt + Scarf + Jeans + Leather Jacket

Create Your Own Formulas

Head into your closet and practice styling outfits using my formulas and any new ones that work for you.

Work

FORMULA #1:

FORMULA #2:

FORMULA #3:

FORMULA #4:

FORMULA #5:

FORMULA #6:

Social

FORMULA #1:

FORMULA #2:

FORMULA #3:

Weekend

FORMULA #1:

FORMULA #2:

FORMULA #3:

Should It Stay or Should It Go?

72-Hour Keep-or-Return Rule

Buying new things can be exhilarating. I believe that level of excitement, at least for me, was programmed at a young age. When my parents bought me a new toy, I promise you that sucker was ripped out of its package by the time we hit the parking lot. So naturally I exhibited the same behavior when it came to buying clothes.

I found myself "popping tags" (then throwing them in the trash) seconds after bringing home a new outfit, only to discover after a few days that I didn't actually love that outfit as much as I thought. Those pieces went on to sit in my closet to die a dusty unworn death. What a giant waste of money. This is exactly why I invented the 72-hour rule.

Now that you've tried on your new clothes with the pieces that you already own and created outfit formulas that work for you, it's time to do the final analysis on what stays and what goes.

Take out everything you've decided is a keeper. Flip back to your Haul Log on pages 146–147 to make notes, and ask yourself the following questions about each garment:

- Do I still love it?

- Does it really fit well, or should I exchange it for another size/get it altered?

- Do I have something exactly like this in my closet already?

- Can I create at least three outfits with this?

WEEK
4

DAY
25

You may realize that something you previously thought was a winner actually has limited use. And from creating your outfit formulas, you might want to go back and shop for a few more versions of an item that is clearly working for you.

Aren't you glad you waited before tearing off those tags?

The Finishing Touches

Apparently, accessories are the scary monsters of the fashion world. I know this because my clients are terrified and bewildered by them. I've cleaned out hundreds of closets, and the majority of them are devoid of accessories. No jewelry, no scarves, no hats, and zero fun belts.

As a cheerleader for accessories, this upsets the heck out of me, because they are clearly the personality of the outfit. It's time to face your fears and start embracing accessories. We'll do it together, one step at a time.

Accessory Checklist

Check off the accessories you'd love to wear and can see yourself incorporating into your everyday look:

[ ] Statement Necklace

[ ] Layered Delicate Necklaces

[ ] Cuff

[ ] Stacked Bracelets

[ ] Cocktail Rings

[ ] Dainty Rings

[ ] Statement Earrings

[ ] Dainty Earrings

[ ] Hat

[ ] Silk Scarf

[ ] Woven Scarf

[ ] Waist-Cinching Belt

[ ] Sunglasses

[ ] Statement Optical Glasses

[ ] Wrap or Pashmina

[ ] Statement Hosiery

[ ] Brooches and Pins

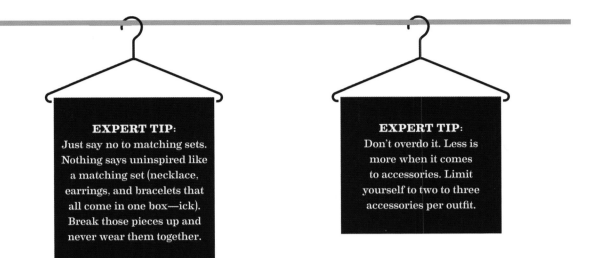

EXPERT TIP:
Just say no to matching sets.
Nothing says uninspired like
a matching set (necklace,
earrings, and bracelets that
all come in one box—ick).
Break those pieces up and
never wear them together.

EXPERT TIP:
Don't overdo it. Less is
more when it comes
to accessories. Limit
yourself to two to three
accessories per outfit.

Accessory Personality Profile

Now check off the accessory personality that speaks to you the most.

[ ] **Artistic/Quirky**
What it looks like: lots of color, layers, and statement pieces

[ ] **Bohemian/Free Spirit**
What it looks like: earthy elements like wood, suede, rope, and fringe

[ ] **Bold/Sexy**
What it looks like: saturated colors, and larger-than-life jewelry

[ ] **Classic/Conservative**
What it looks like: timeless elements like pearls, diamond studs, and silk scarves

[ ] **Edgy/Rocker**
What it looks like: Think spikes, studs, leather, and chains.

[ ] **Elegant/Sophisticated**
What it looks like: diamonds, chandelier earrings, and cocktail rings

[ ] **Relaxed/Easygoing**
What it looks like: woven scarves, dainty jewelry, and casual hats

[ ] **Sporty/Athletic**
What it looks like: baseball caps, watches, and woven or plastic jewelry

WEEK
4

DAY
26

Accessorizing Like a Pro

Style four outfits that include at least two accessories. Snap photos and tape them here.

OUTFIT #1

OUTFIT #2

THIS OUTFIT WOULD BE PERFECT FOR:

_____

_____

_____

_____

THIS OUTFIT WOULD BE PERFECT FOR:

_____

_____

_____

_____

OUTFIT #3

OUTFIT #4

THIS OUTFIT WOULD BE PERFECT FOR:

_____

_____

_____

_____

_____

THIS OUTFIT WOULD BE PERFECT FOR:

_____

_____

_____

_____

_____

Exiting Your Comfort Zone

As we near the end of this style journey, I think it's safe to say that you've come a long way. You've developed your unique sense of style, you're shopping like a pro, and you're accessorizing like a champ, but I have the sneaking suspicion that you're still holding back.

There have been plenty of times in my life when I swore I was really going for it, but deep down inside I knew I had more. It was a lingering out-of-focus feeling of doubt, unworthiness, and discomfort. The picture didn't become clear until I read the book *The Big Leap* by Gay Hendricks.

The Big Leap describes something called the "Upper Limit Problem," where we reach a certain level of success and then unknowingly self-sabotage ourselves (like getting out of debt and celebrating by buying an expensive present). All of this occurs because where we came from— as much as we wanted to leave it—was comfortable. It's called our comfort zone, and just as the motivational crowd loves to say, "Nothing great happens in your comfort zone."

It's time to squeeze the last bit of juice out of that orange. If you're holding back on fully expressing yourself through style, now is the time to break through. Anytime you're feeling pulled back into your comfort zone, bust out one of these mini styling challenges to get you back on track.

Challenge #1: Try a half tuck (tucking in part of your shirt for waist definition and instant cool).

Challenge #2: Make a statement with jewelry.

Challenge #3: Rock red lipstick.

Challenge #4: Wear a pair of sneakers with a dress.

Challenge #5: Try out a new 'do.

Challenge #6: Swap out your blazer for a leather jacket.

Challenge #7: Layer a blouse under a dress.

DAY 27: DO THE WORK

Get Honest

REFLECT ON IT: Look at the work you've done so far. Where are you still holding back?

_____

_____

_____

LEAN INTO IT: Is there a particular garment or styling technique you're still too afraid to try?

_____

_____

_____

ADDRESS IT: Are there some lingering roadblocks that still need your attention?

_____

_____

_____

PLAY AROUND: Did you learn anything from trying one of the mini challenges on the previous page?

_____

_____

_____

Create Your Look Book

I'm the kind of gal who needs a plan for everything.
I am the polar opposite of carefree, flying by the seat of
my pants. Give me structure or give me death. Go ahead
and call me rigid, I don't care, because at the end of the
day, planning pays—especially when it comes to style.

Without planning, I instantly lose my style street cred.
I default to jeans and a T-shirt just like the rest of them.
The key to my style success is planning out all of my
outfits ahead of time. I've been doing this since high
school.

The night before school I'd carefully plan out my look and
place it at the foot of my bed. That way, when I woke up,
I could easily get dressed and know that I looked good.
However, when I failed to plan ahead, I was sure to have a
closet meltdown.

Closet Meltdown: throwing a crazy tantrum in your
closet while trying to find something to wear. Side effects
include tears, clothes all of the floor, and screaming.

**I don't want you to have a closet meltdown ever again. I
want you to feel confident every time you walk out the
door. Here is how we're going to do it.**

STEP #1:

Set aside the time.

Every Sunday I block off at least an hour for outfit planning. I look at my calendar and see what's on the agenda that week so that I'm guaranteed to have the right looks at the ready.

STEP #2:

Make it fun.

I put on my favorite movie in the background or a Netflix comedy special. Have a glass of wine, a piece of candy . . . whatever you need to do to make this an experience something you look forward to.

STEP #3:

Pick 7 pieces.

Whenever I'm styling an outfit, I like to start with the "hero" piece, aka the garment that I want to be the star of ensemble.

STEP #4:

Style, snap, and repeat.

Take your hero piece and build your look around it, trying different outfit formulas until you get it just right. When you land on your winning look, snap a selfie and repeat the process for each hero piece.

STEP #5:

Create your look book.

Use the outfit-planning template below or create an album in your phone with all of your outfit pics. Remember, it's 100 percent A-OK to repeat outfits, so keep those photos handy for the days when you're too busy to preplan.

WEEK

4

DAY

28

DAY 28: DO THE WORK
Look #1

TOP

_____
_____
_____

BOTTOM

_____
_____
_____

DRESS/JUMPSUIT

_____
_____
_____

ACCESSORIES

_____
_____

SHOES

_____
_____

APPROPRIATE FOR:

☐ **Work**   ☐ **Weekend**   ☐ **Social**

Look #2

TOP

_____

_____

_____

_____

BOTTOM

_____

_____

_____

_____

DRESS/JUMPSUIT

_____

_____

_____

ACCESSORIES

_____

_____

SHOES

_____

_____

WEEK
4

DAY
28

APPROPRIATE FOR:

☐ **Work**   ☐ **Weekend**   ☐ **Social**

Look #3

DATE: / /

TOP

BOTTOM

DRESS/JUMPSUIT

ACCESSORIES

SHOES

APPROPRIATE FOR:

☐ **Work**   ☐ **Weekend**   ☐ **Social**

Look #4

TOP

_____

_____

_____

_____

BOTTOM

_____

_____

_____

DRESS/JUMPSUIT

_____

_____

_____

_____

ACCESSORIES

_____

_____

SHOES

_____

_____

WEEK
4

DAY
28

APPROPRIATE FOR:

☐ **Work**   ☐ **Weekend**   ☐ **Social**

Look #5

TOP

BOTTOM

DRESS/JUMPSUIT

ACCESSORIES

SHOES

APPROPRIATE FOR:

☐ **Work**   ☐ **Weekend**   ☐ **Social**

Look #6

TOP

BOTTOM

DRESS/JUMPSUIT

ACCESSORIES

SHOES

WEEK
4

DAY
28

APPROPRIATE FOR:

☐ **Work**   ☐ **Weekend**   ☐ **Social**

Look #7

TOP

_____

_____

_____

BOTTOM

_____

_____

_____

DRESS/JUMPSUIT

_____

_____

_____

ACCESSORIES

_____

_____

SHOES

_____

_____

APPROPRIATE FOR:

☐ **Work**   ☐ **Weekend**   ☐ **Social**

Look #8

TOP

_____

_____

_____

BOTTOM

_____

_____

_____

DRESS/JUMPSUIT

_____

_____

_____

ACCESSORIES

_____

_____

SHOES

_____

_____

APPROPRIATE FOR:

☐ **Work**   ☐ **Weekend**   ☐ **Social**

WEEK
4

DAY
28

Celebrating Your After

As a person who is passionate about winning (seriously, I've flipped tables during game night), allow me to be the first to high-five you as you cross the finish line. You did it! Almost everyone wants a taste of sweet, sweet victory, but it takes a certain kind of person to make it to the end.

But here's the thing. Most high-achieving winners rarely celebrate their wins. Myself included. There have been plenty of goals I dreamed of achieving, and when I finally achieved them, I was like, "All right, what's next?" It's only during those moments of reflection that I can really appreciate how far I've come.

You've come a long way since our first day together. So let's collectively do better and celebrate this massive victory. Because if you don't celebrate it, who will? Well, besides me, but that's like your mother being proud of you. Of course she's proud; she's your mom.

How will you celebrate your transformation? How about treating yourself to one of these:

- An investment piece for your wardrobe

- A spa day or a mani-pedi

- A nice dinner out with friends or family

- A luxury staycation

I have no shortage of ideas for you. Please, please, please promise that you'll take a victory lap after all of the work you've done this month.

Get Ready for Your Big Reveal

Reflect and Celebrate

You can't see how far you've come if you don't remember where you came from. Go ahead and stick your very first selfie here:

Before

WHAT I WORE:

HOW I FELT:

Now put your best outfit on and snap your jaw-dropping "after" here:

Before

WHAT I'M WEARING:

_____

_____

_____

_____

_____

_____

_____

_____

_____

_____

_____

HOW I FEEL NOW:

_____

_____

_____

_____

Post-Challenge Reflections

ON A SCALE FROM 1–10, how satisfied are you with your personal style now?

1   2   3   4   5   6   7   8   9   10

Remember the intention you set at the beginning of this process? Did you achieve your desired outcome?

_____

_____

_____

_____

_____

_____

_____

List three positive things that have happened as a result of improving your style:

1. _____

2. _____

3. _____

How have you changed since improving your sense of style?

_____

_____

_____

_____

_____

_____

Has getting dressed become easier since the beginning of this process?

_____

_____

_____

_____

_____

How confident are you that you can reach your personal and professional goals since improving your style?

_____

_____

_____

_____

_____

Write a Letter to Yourself

Close out this book by writing a letter to yourself reflecting on and celebrating your 30-day style journey.

Make a promise to yourself to maintain your new look and continue to update your style as you evolve.

Dear _____ ,

You did it! You completed your 30-day journey to self-discovery and style. How does it feel? _____

_____

_____

From this point on, you will do whatever it takes to hold true to the new vision you created for yourself.

That means you will wear clothes that make you feel _____ , and people will perceive you as a _____ , _____ , and _____ woman.

In order to lock this magic in, you're going to sign a contract with yourself: I, _____ agree on this _____ day of _____ 20 _____ , to maintain my new and improved sense of style. I will stay focused on the vision I have designed for myself and my life. I promise to update my style as I evolve and grow.

NAME: _____   **DATE:** _____

SIGNATURE: _____

It's So Hard to Say Goodbye

Let's Keep in Touch

You—yes, you—are the whole reason I got into this line of work. Your transformations are inspiring and need to be shared.

I want to see how <u>Style Therapy</u> has impacted your life. Share your stories, your before and after pics, and your wins on social media. Tag me, @laurenmessiah, on Instagram and use the hashtag #LMStyleTherapy so I can help celebrate your new look.

Remember, when you share your <u>Style Therapy</u> stories, you not only put a smile on my face, you inspire other women to show up as their best, most awesome selves too.

By the way, this style party doesn't have to end here. Let's keep the momentum going by joining the community! Style Confidence Collective is the place to be if you want to discover yourself and your style, and reach your full potential. Visit LaurenMessiah.com/collective.

Next, take your styling skills to the next level with Personal Style University. Learn how to style yourself like a pro with advanced styling lessons and techniques. Visit LaurenMessiah.com/PSU to learn more.

And finally, I have a ton of free videos on my YouTube channel. Go ahead and get your subscribe on at YouTube.com/laurenmessiah so you won't miss a single video.

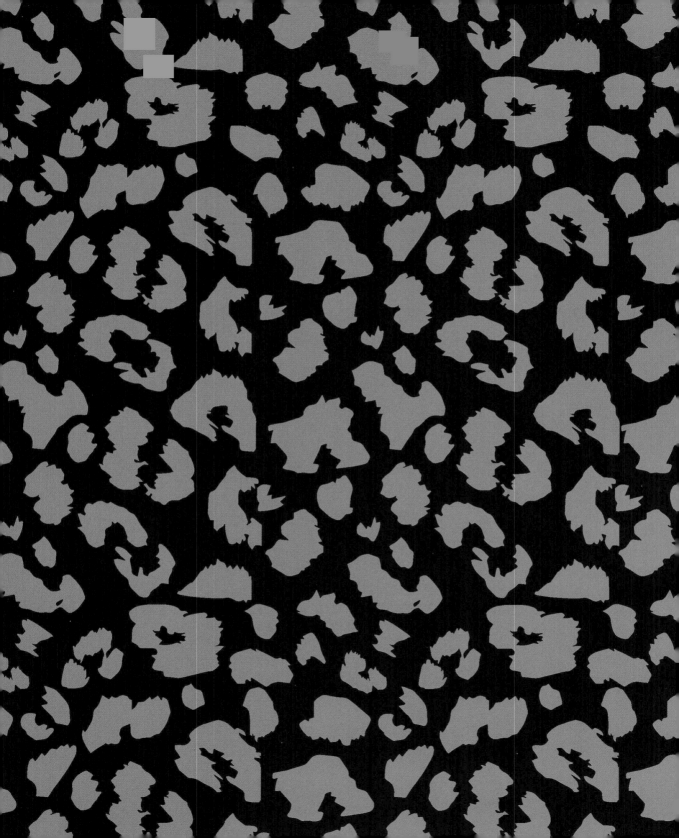

Additional
Resources

Dressing for Body Confidence

Clients often want the rules for choosing clothes that flatter their shape. The truth is that body-type dressing can be confusing even for a stylist. For one thing, fashion trends are always changing. A new silhouette comes along and suddenly it challenges what we previously assumed was flattering.

What we're aiming for is body confidence for all shapes and sizes. Some days, that might mean choosing clothes that balance the proportions of your body. Other days, you might go for a look that exaggerates one aspect of your shape.

The tips I'm sharing here are useful if your aim is to balance the upper and lower halves of the body. Please use them at your discretion and whatever you do, don't get hung up on doing this "perfectly."

Style Space Fillers

Here are some tools you can use to fill out or amplify parts of your body:

- Bright and bold colors
- Loud or vibrant prints
- Shine (sequins, metallics)
- Texture (chunky knits, tweed)
- Strategically placed pockets
- Shoulder pads
- Ruffles and bows

Style Space Reducers

Here are some tools you can use to minimize parts of your body:

- Solid colors
- Dark colors
- Neutral colors
- Structured fabrics
- Smaller prints that will "confuse" the eye
- Belts

If you want to . . .

Balance a Bigger Top Half

WHAT WORKS:
- Supportive bras
- Tops with wide straps
- Tops with an open neck (V-neck, cowl neck, scoop neck)
- Voluminous skirts
- Printed pants and skirts
- Wide-leg or flare-cut pants

WHAT DOESN'T:
- Tops that are too skimpy/revealing
- Baggy tops and dresses
- Spaghetti straps
- Tops with large ruffles and bows
- Super-skinny jeans
- Overly tight/slim-cut skirts
- High-necked tops and turtlenecks

Minimize the Middle

WHAT WORKS:

- Trouser cut and wide-leg pants
- A-line skirts and dresses
- V-neck tops (the deeper, the better)
- Single-button jackets
- Belts to place around the smallest part of your waist
- An open jacket or blazer over a darker top

WHAT DOESN'T:

- Skinny jeans and leggings
- Three-button jackets
- Low-rise jeans (a higher rise holds in the tummy)

Emphasize an Hourglass

WHAT WORKS:

- Waist-defining belts
- Fit-and-flare dresses
- Pencil skirts that hit right above the knee
- Garments that fit close to the body
- Tailored garments with plenty of structure
- Wrap dresses

WHAT DOESN'T:

- Shapeless tops
- Tent dresses
- Micro-miniskirts
- Plunging necklines

Balance a Bigger Bottom Half

WHAT WORKS:

- Printed tops
- Tops with fun details like ruffles or embellishments
- Structured jackets and blazers
- Dark streamlined pants and skirts

WHAT DOESN'T:

- Printed jeans
- Pants and skirts in bold colors
- Heavy materials on the bottom half, like tweed
- Long tops and tunics that cover your hips
- Three-dimensional details (like patch pockets) on the bottom-half

Create an Illusion of Curves

WHAT WORKS:

- Garments with strategic seaming (like princess seams)
- Knits and other figure-hugging materials
- Backless garments
- Plunging necklines
- Ruffles, pockets, and three-dimensional details

WHAT DOESN'T:

- Garments that you can't "fill out"
- Overly baggy clothing

Tailoring

For some crazy reason, most of the women I encounter resist going to the tailor (like, hard-core resist). Instead they take on the "nothing ever fits me" mentality, beat themselves up for not fitting into clothing directly off the rack, and give up on looking good. Well, I have news for you: The majority of women (well over 60 percent) can't waltz into a boutique and find something that fits perfectly.

You are not alone.

Developing a relationship with a tailor is key. For a few extra bucks, your clothes will fit better and your confidence will soar. Still intimidated? I get it. The two biggest fears when visiting a tailor for the first time are:

1. What if they butcher my clothes?

2. Will it cost me a fortune?

To answer point number one, I'm going to share the mother of all tips for finding the best tailors in your city. Call the fanciest boutique or department store in your city and ask where they take their alterations. The best stylists in Hollywood use this technique to find tailors for their A-list clients. If you're still nervous, start with an inexpensive garment to test out their skills before going whole hog with the good stuff.

And to answer the "Will it cost me a fortune?" question, check out my tailoring cost sheet here. The cost breakdown is based on a tailor I visit in Los Angeles. The costs may vary from tailor to tailor, but this guide will at least give you a ballpark estimate on what you're going to spend.

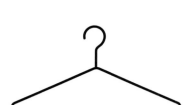

EXPERT TIP:
When hemming jeans, always make sure they use the original hem. This will give you a more polished look. Trust me, it's worth the extra couple of bucks.

Tailoring Cost Sheet

BLAZERS, SUITS, JACKETS

Shorten or lengthen sleeves: $20

Remove buttonholes: $10

Take sides in or out: $20

Take center seam in or out: $15

Adjust center seam with vent: $18

Raise or shorten back: $24

Add shoulder pads: $15

Add facing: $10

Move buttons: $1 per button

COATS AND OUTERWEAR

Shorten sleeves: $18

Shorten sleeves with cuff,
belt, or details: $25

Take sides in or out: $25

Add facing: $10

SHIRTS AND BLOUSES

Make long-sleeve shirt short: $12

Shorten sleeves and move placket: $20

Shorten or lengthen
sleeves without placket: $12

Taper sleeves/take in sleeve width: $20

Add darts: $10

PANTS AND SLACKS

Hem unfinished/open bottom: $10

Hem finished bottom: $15

Reattach original denim/jeans hem: $22

Hem hand-finished (for delicate fabrics): $24

Waist taken in or out with waistband split: $15

Waist taken in or out with waistband removal: $22

Waist, seat, and thigh adjustments: $24

Seat taken in, shaped, or deepened: $10

Taper leg: $20

Line crotch: $15

Replace zipper: $17

Add facing: $10

Recut: $60

SKIRTS AND DRESSES

Hem, shorten, or lengthen: $22

Hem partial pleating: $30

Full pleat hem: $42

Shorten or lengthen sleeves on dress: $17

Shorten sleeves and move placket: $20

Taper dress sleeves: $17

Take in waist: $22

Take out waist (add fabric): $25

Take in sides with pockets: $20

Take in sides without pockets: $16

Add facing: $10

Wardrobe Tools and Essentials

A stylist wouldn't dream of dressing a client without her kit. This grab bag full of goodies is a nonnegotiable when it comes to nailing the style game. Now, I don't recommend you lug around a fifty-pound bag of styling gear, but there are a few must-haves you'll need in order to make your closet complete.

The Work Kit

Fashion emergencies are never fun, but they are even less fun when the style drama goes down in the office. Grab a small makeup bag, fill it with items below, pop it in your desk drawer, and you'll be good to go!

- Safety pins
- Travel sewing kit
- Lint brush
- Tide To-Go Pen
- Static Guard
- Clear nail polish (for stocking runs)

- Spare earring backs
- Double-sided tape (for hems that come unstitched)
- Emergency hygiene and beauty products (tampon, mints, floss, deodorant wipes, nail polish remover wipes, lip balm)

For Special Occasions

A night out on the town while dressed in your evening finest requires "fashion emergency" equipment fit for an A-lister. Keep these items in your closet or tucked away in your lingerie drawer to avoid any fashion faux pas.

- Double-sided styling tape
- Stick-on bra (for backless dresses)
- Nipple covers
- Sweat protectors

- Moleskin
- Shoe inserts and heel pads
- Spanx and body shapers
- Bra strap converters

Closet Equipment

If I had a quarter for every closet I worked in that had <u>nothing</u> from this list, I'd be doing coin-operated laundry for life. Some of the items on this list may feel a little intimidating or advanced—don't worry, you can work up to those. However, if you see a little asterisk by an item on this list, it means you should've purchased it yesterday.

- Full-length mirror*
- Clothing steamer (handheld or standing)*
- Garment rack
- Slim-line hangers*
- Pant hangers*
- Cedar (to keep the moths away)*
- Charcoal air-purifying bags (great for keeping your sock drawer fresh)
- Hanging jewelry organizer
- Jewelry displays
- Drawer organizers for undergarments and hosiery
- Rack dividers for organizing your closet/ daily outfits

Laundry Gear

We'll get into the actual doing of the laundry on page 190, but in the meantime, you may as well stock up on the goods. I realize this isn't going to be like buying a jug of Tide at Target, but spending a little extra money up front will save from ruined clothing and crazy dry-cleaning bills.

- Specialty detergent for lingerie*
- Specialty detergent for wool and cashmere*
- Sweater drying rack
- Wool or plastic dryer balls
- Iron cleaner
- Mesh laundry bag for lingerie
- Divided laundry hamper (separate those lights and darks)
- Shout Wipe & Go wipes
- Tide To Go pen

*The brand The Laundress makes really awesome specialty detergents for denim, wool, cashmere, and workout clothes. Their products are definitely a splurge, but if you really care about a particular garment, it's worth it.

Fabric Care

When it comes to taking care of your clothing, do I as I say and not as I do, because I'm the queen of "let's roll the dice" on this one. I'm 100 percent the girl who doesn't separate her lights and darks. I ruined my brand-new white jeans last week because I tossed a tie-dye hoodie in there at the same time. But you worked too hard building your perfect wardrobe to throw it away with careless laundry habits.

First, let's get the "big duh" tips out of the way, shall we?

Separate your lights and darks, and never take a gamble on red garments. Wash those suckers alone.

When in doubt, just take it to the dry cleaner.

All right, now that we've got that out of the way, let's move on to a few key fabric care tips.

Fabric Care Guide

COTTON

These days most cotton garments are preshrunk, so don't take up a lot of mental space worrying about shrinking a garment. Machine wash using cold or warm water with standard detergent.

POLYESTER, NYLON, SPANDEX, ACRYLIC, AND ACETATE

These synthetics won't shrink, and they naturally resist any water-based stains. Many of these fabrics produce static and may permanently wrinkle if placed in a hot dryer (no, keep that baby on low). Machine wash these garments using warm water and regular detergent. A little fabric softener will help with the static. Save money and the environment by using dryer balls instead of dryer sheets.

WOOL

If you're one of the lucky ones who doesn't itch like crazy when your skin comes in contact with wool, let's celebrate and care for it properly. Wool is ultra-durable, but it does shrink in warm water. Keep your wool right-sized by hand-washing in cold water with a mild detergent, or just take it the dry cleaner. Air-dry your wool using a stackable drying rack. Then store with cedar to keep the moths away.

SILK

Silk is fancy, delicate, and easy to ruin, so please, please, please dry-clean all of your silk garments. If you're a risk-taker, you can hand-wash your silks in cold water with a mild detergent. If you spill anything oily on silk, immediately hit it with some baby powder. The powder will soak up the oil, but it's best to follow up with a trip to the dry cleaner to completely remove the stain.

RAYON

Rayon is a seminatural fabric, meaning it has natural and synthetic fibers. This is also means it's tricky. Rayon is at risk for color bleeding, shrinking, or just losing its general freshness. Dry-clean or hand-wash in cold water with a mild detergent to keep it in good shape. When dealing with rayon wrinkles, it's best to iron while the garment is still slightly damp.

LINEN

Linen wrinkles easier than your fingers after an hour-long bath, so ironing is a requirement (steaming isn't strong enough). Take your linen to the dry cleaner or hand-wash in cold water with a mild detergent. Air-dry only! If you don't want to spend the extra cash at the dry cleaner, you can machine wash linen—just make sure you run the gentle cycle.

Editor: Karrie Witkin
Designer: Melissa Faustine
Production Manager: Rebecca Westall
Photography: Drea Castro

ISBN: 978-1-4197-4546-1

Printed and bound in China
10 9 8 7 6 5 4 3 2

Abrams Image products are available at special discounts when
purchased in quantity for premiums and promotions as well as fundraising
or educational use. Special editions can also be created to specification.
For details, contact specialsales@abramsbooks.com or the address below.

ABRAMS The Art of Books
195 Broadway, New York, NY 10007
abramsbooks.com